To Budd &
my wonderful in-laws—
wishing you the Best
of everything, today,
tomorrow + always.
your loving
Son - in - law,

Tim
2-23-08

The Secret Science of Price and Volume

Founded in 1807, John Wiley & Sons is the oldest independent publishing company in the United States. With offices in North America, Europe, Australia and Asia, Wiley is globally committed to developing and marketing print and electronic products and services for our customers' professional and personal knowledge and understanding.

The Wiley Trading series features books by traders who have survived the market's ever changing temperament and have prospered—some by reinventing systems, others by getting back to basics. Whether a novice trader, professional or somewhere in-between, these books will provide the advice and strategies needed to prosper today and well into the future.

For a list of available titles, please visit our web site at www.WileyFinance.com.

The Secret Science of Price and Volume

Techniques for Spotting Market Trends, Hot Sectors, and the Best Stocks

TIMOTHY ORD

WILEY

John Wiley & Sons, Inc.

Published by John Wiley & Sons, Inc., Hoboken, New Jersey.
Published simultaneously in Canada.

For general information on our other products and services or for technical support, please contact our Customer Care Department within the United States at (800) 762-2974, outside the United States at (317) 572-3993 or fax (317) 572-4002.

Wiley also publishes its books in a variety of electronic formats. Some content that appears in print may not be available in electronic formats. For more information about Wiley products, visit our web site at www.wiley.com.

Library of Congress Cataloging-in-Publication Data:

Ord, Timothy, 1949-
  The secret science of price and volume techniques for spotting market trends, hot sectors, and the best stocks / Timothy Ord.
      p.   cm.—(Wiley trading series)
  Includes index.
    ISBN 978-0-470-13898-4 (cloth)
      1. Stocks—Prices.   2. Investments.   3. Speculation.   I. Title.
HG4636.O73 2008
332.63'2042—dc22

                                                              2007032150

Printed in the United States of America

10   9   8   7   6   5   4   3   2   1

Contents

Preface

I always had a fascination for numbers, and I graduated from the University of Nebraska with a teaching degree in mathematics. When I changed careers (as I will relate in Chapter 1), I became a stockbroker in the late 1970s. The brokerage firm I worked for believed in fundamentals only. When it came to the stock price moving up or down, they thought it was only due to the balance sheets, earnings, management, and so forth. Because of this belief, the brokerage company had an extensive fundamental research department that gave its opinions on numerous stocks.

One particular time I remember well, the research department had a long-term bearish view of Teledyne Technologies. At the time, Teledyne had been gradually moving down for several months. I showed this report to one of my clients who owned that stock. Because of this bearish fundamental report, my client sold his shares. Just days after the client sold, shares of Teledyne started a rally that would continue for more than a year, resulting in a gain of over 300 percent. How had the fundamental research department been so wrong?

I knew the brokerage firm stressed fundamentals, which they believed was the only way to pick stocks. As far as they were concerned, technical analysis was only for witchdoctors and sorcerers, who would take bones out of a pouch and throw them on the ground and then pick stocks depending on the way the bones fell. When I studied my firm's fundamental researcher reports for a while, however, I found that a lot of times they were 180 degrees off the true trend of the stock. I became disenchanted with stock picking based on fundamentals and started to turn my attention to technical analysis for choosing stocks. To this day, I don't like to hear the word *fundamental*, because I know now that fundamentally stocks appear the worst at their bottoms and best at their tops.

About this time, I started to read market letters by Joe Granville and Stan Weinstein, who were two leading market technicians at the time. Now these guys had something I could wrap my mind around! It was all about numbers when it came to finding market direction and stock picking. With my mathematics degree, I know that numbers are what we can use to prove facts or deny a fallacy. To me, fundamental research is nothing more than opinion, which I see as the downfall of that type of analysis.

After I moved to Colorado around 1980 I started to work for a brokerage company that appreciated my work in technical analysis. I was still in the early learning stages of becoming a technician; nonetheless, I was probably the best technician at that firm at the time. In these early years I developed a tick index trading method that worked well in picking short-term tops and bottoms in the market. I used this method to trade puts and calls on the OEX (S&P 100 Index) as well as to time trades in options on stocks.

My business grew in option trading, and the firm I was working for made me the option principal and vice president. In 1989 and the early 1990s, I wrote a couple of articles about the tick index trading method for *Stock & Commodities* magazine. The short-term tick index method is still being used today by traders and has stood the test of time.

By the late 1980s, I had reached a level where I was fairly efficient in trading. I had also started my own market letter called *The Ord Oracle*. At times, I would go for months with hardly a losing trade, and at other times, I would struggle. What I did not understand at the time was that short-term trading works well if the trend is in your favor, but not so well if it is not. This little bit of knowledge took several more years to realize. By the mid-1990s, it had become very clear to me that to be successful in the market a high percentage of the time, a trader must know what direction the general market was heading and then trade that direction. Thinking back on my trading career, I would have saved lots of time, energy, and money if I had known this simple step in trading. There are probably thousands of trading methods out there, and most will work just fine if they are aligned with the market.

Throughout this book, I will cover simple techniques—the types that make you slap your palm to your forehead and say, "I should have thought of that!" As you will read, many of the techniques presented in this book involve a common-sense approach to market timing and trading. (One of my more important techniques is the "Wind at Your Back" method of making sure you are aligned with the overall trend of the market.) I also present a new trading technique for stock and indexes that involves price and volume, which I named *Ord-Volume*. I believe traders will find it interesting.

The most difficult thing I ask traders to do is have patience, to wait for the trade to be aligned with the market. If a trader can master patience, then he or she will be more likely to have great success in the markets. I had to learn patience myself, and often I was taught that lesson the hard way. My goal in this book is to help traders shorten their learning curves in order to become more successful in the market.

TIMOTHY G. ORD
The Ord Oracle
www.Ord-Oracle.com

This book is dedicated to my Christian faith that has lighted my path to life; to my wife, Dawn, who has stayed by my side in good times and bad and in sickness and health; and to our wonderful loving daughter, Heather.

Acknowledgments

First, I must thank my loving wife, Dawn, who encouraged me and set up the opportunity to speak with my publisher, John Wiley & Sons, to write this book. Without her persistence in this matter, there most likely would have been a long delay in the writing of this book.

I also wish to thank Fari Hamzei (www.HamzeiAnalytics.com), who chose me to be among more than a dozen other traders, money managers, and analysts who wrote chapters for his book, *Master Traders: Strategies for Superior Returns from Today's Top Traders* (John Wiley & Sons, 2006). Thank you, Fari, for giving me that opportunity, which, in turn, opened the door for my own book.

Kevin Commins, senior acquisition editor at Wiley, first embraced the concept of this book, and Emilie Herman, senior development editor, shepherded every chapter and graphic along the way. Thank you for your support and patience.

Patricia Crisafulli, my personal editor for this book, carefully and masterfully helped me to write in a way that would make the most sense to readers. You are a pleasure to work with, Tricia.

George and Ellen, my parents, were wonderful people who instilled in me a strong work ethic and a "never give up" attitude. They both have passed away, God bless them, and I am grateful for their positive influence in my life. My brother Dan, who got me started and "showed me the way."

And to the University of Nebraska, which gave me a wonderful education. Go Huskers!

All the Best,
Timothy G. Ord

About the Author

Tim Ord has been a respected figure in the financial industry for more than 25 years. A University of Nebraska graduate (1973) with a bachelor of science teaching degree in mathematics, he also held the Series 7, 63, 4 and 24 brokerage licenses. In his career, he has held several positions with financial services and brokerage firms, including as vice president and option principal.

Tim placed fourth nationally in the United States Trading Championship in 1988 in the option division. In 2002, Tim placed ninth in total returns with Schreiner Capital, a money management firm, out of 294 money managers.

He is frequently among the top ten timers rated by *Timer Digest*. He placed fifth for the six months ended October 9, 2006, for the S&P 500. He was the number one gold timer ranked by *Timer Digest* for the year ending January 13, 2006.

Tim writes and publishes the respected market letter *The Ord Oracle* (www.ord-oracle.com), which he founded in 1990. *The Ord Oracle* market letter is e-mailed four days a week, Monday through Thursday, and covers the S&P, Nasdaq, and the gold market.

In the early 1990s, Tim introduced a new trading method using the New York Stock Exchange tick index combined with candlestick charting, which is now used worldwide by short-term traders. He published several articles on the methodology in *Technical Analysis of Stocks & Commodities* magazine in the early to mid-1990s. This method is now used worldwide by short-term traders. Tim has also published on other topics in *Technical Analysis of Stocks & Commodities*, including his July 2005 article in which he discussed the trading rules he developed using price and volume.

In 2004, Tim developed a software program for stocks and index trading that uses the volume strength in a swing to determine buy and sell signals. Tim calls his software program *Ord-Volume* and is actively marketing it worldwide. He has given numerous seminars from coast to coast along with lectures to financial groups.

For more information, please see his web site at www.ord-oracle .com, or e-mail him at Tim@Ord-Oracle.com.

CHAPTER 1

My Path to Successful Trading

My path to successful trading has been anything but smooth. Along the way there have been many twists, wrong turns, obstacles, and potholes. Looking back on my career, I can see that I learned from my mistakes just as much as from my successes—perhaps even more. What made a difference was my willingness to following my dream, to chart my own course, if you will. I knew what I wanted (at least most of the time), and one opportunity led me to the next.

Over the course of my trading career to date, I've been a stockbroker as well as a market analyst, specializing in technical analysis. Through careful study of the market, along with a good deal of diligence and persistence and maybe even a little luck, I have achieved some success— including national *Timer Digest* rankings for both the Standard & Poor's (S&P) 500 Index and in the gold market. I am the president, editor, and publisher of *The Ord Oracle*, my newsletter on the S&P, Nasdaq, and gold issues, which I established in 1990.

From the time I began in the market as a stockbroker in the 1980s through the present day, I have been a student of the market, learning from books, courses, other traders, and even from my customers. If you keep your eyes and your mind open, you'll be rewarded with many lessons and experiences. In trading, it is essential, and in life it certainly makes things interesting.

I grew up on a farm in a small town called Beatrice, Nebraska, population 12,130. Before my high school graduation in 1967, the school's career counselor called a meeting with my parents and me. I told him that my plans were to go to college. The counselor, however, advised my parents that I would not last three months in college and told them not to waste the money. The military, he said, was a better option, and suggested the Army as a good choice and the infantry as the best division for me. Obviously displeased with my antics in high school, the counselor thought that I needed discipline, and the Army would teach me that.

However, I did go to college and I did last more than three months. As a matter of fact, I spent six years, graduating in 1973 from the University of Nebraska, with a teaching degree in mathematics. This choice of study would prove fortuitous later on as a technical analyst, although in the short term it had some drawbacks. At the time I went to college, there was a teacher shortage, so much so that the government gave financial incentives to students entering teaching programs in the 1960s. That financial incentive drew a lot of students to teaching, so that by the time I graduated from college there was a mass of new teachers, and the market was flooded. (Funny how government incentives work, isn't it?)

Unless you had a parent who was a principal somewhere who could get you a job, back then you were an unemployed teacher. I did find a job at the Nebraska State Prison as a prison counselor and worked there for nearly three years. (The prison job is an interesting story unto itself, but that will get me off the subject of my path to successful trading.) Suffice it to say that, while the prison job was interesting, I was seeking something more financially rewarding. One of my very good friends at the time had just gone to work for a brokerage firm, and he had a lot of good things to say about his new job. Hearing him talk, I kept telling myself, "I could do this. I know a lot about 'stocks.' I was raised on a farm and I was around cattle all my life, so I know stock!" (If you haven't caught on already, I was thinking of the livestock variety.)

Buoyed with confidence, I went out and interviewed with a different brokerage firm than where my friend worked and ended up in Omaha with a job at one of the major wire houses at that time. I was sent to San Francisco to receive my education and training and to pass the National Association of Securities Dealers (NASD) Series 7 examination to become a licensed stockbroker. I passed the exam and came back to Omaha to start my new job.

BECOMING A BROKER

I thought that clients would be lined up at my door and that orders would be flowing into my office. Not the case—not the case at all. As a new broker, I made cold calls—from the phonebook—all day. This was not what I had envisioned. However, I did make a decent living, and my lifestyle improved to the point that I owned a new three-bedroom condominium and I drove a fancy sports car. Life was good.

I became dissatisfied, however, not with the job itself but rather with the management. I didn't like the idea of someone watching every move I made: how many phone calls I made, how much time I spent on the phone with potential clients, whether my coffee break lasted 10 minutes or 20. . . . I wanted something where being managed was not an issue. I heard about being an independent contractor broker, which would mean paying my own expenses and sharing office space with other brokers. There was no management at all; independent brokers came and went as they pleased, as long as they paid their share of the expenses. Omaha did not offer this opportunity, but several brokerage firms in Colorado did. So I sold my condo, packed up my belongings, and moved to Colorado, where I got a job with a firm that had several offices throughout the country with about 200 independent brokers.

Within a couple of years I had become vice president and senior option principal for this firm. Life was good again. This time frame was the late 1970s and into the early 1980s, when the "Elliott Wave" technical analysis fad was becoming popular, along with W. D. Gann trading methods. Explained simply, Elliott Wave is a form of technical analysis theorized by Ralph Nelson Elliott, who believed that market action unfolds in specific wavelike patterns. W. D. Gann was a famous stock and commodity trader, who based his forecasts on time and price. Hearing about Elliott Wave and Gann got me very interested in technical analysis; although I was by no means good at it in the beginning, I was better than most at the time. Majoring in mathematics in college hadn't landed me a teaching job, but it was about to play a very important role in my future career.

FIRST FORAY INTO TECHNICAL ANALYSIS

I did face one big drawback as I began my foray into technical analysis. Back then, computers were very expensive and you needed to be a programmer to run one. Needless to say, I did not have a computer at my disposal. Instead, like a lot of people in the markets in those days, I had to rely on printed charts of stocks and indexes that were sold by companies. The information would be updated through Friday's close and mailed over the weekend. Then, during the week, you had to update the charts by hand. Back then, I used simple moving averages and basic patterns such as "head and shoulders," "triangles," and such.

I also subscribed to several leading market letters, including Robert Prechter and Joe Granville. I wasn't so much interested in the trades they recommended, but rather how they came to the conclusions of what was bearish or bullish. At this early time in my career, charts looked like a bunch of random lines and did not have a definite meaning. Trading felt to me like standing on a very high ledge with wind blowing in every direction, threatening to throw me off balance and cause me to lose my footing—in other words, stressful. I did have my trading winning streaks where it seemed I could do no wrong. However, I would blow myself up with losses that wiped out my profits and would have to regroup.

Several brokers in our offices had an interest in what I was doing and asked me to share my ideas on the markets. I remember talking to several of them in the reception area after the market close one day about how I would convey my ideas in a timely fashion and what to name this service. The most-liked name for this new service was "Timothy's Timely Tips," and it was decided I should provide access to my market messages through my answering machine. So at the end of each day, I put my market message on the answering machine, and the brokers would call the answering machine and instead of hearing, "You have reached the so-and-so residence," they would hear my market message. My answering machine had a one-minute message length, so my market message could not be longer than that.

By this time, I was considered to be the "guru" in this brokerage company, although I was still not up to par as far as my trading was concerned. Still, I did have my moments, all the while searching for the proverbial "Holy Grail" of technical analysis. Also during this time, I met the most beautiful woman. She was hired by the brokerage firm to help run the back office, which handled customer trade confirmations. My first encounter with her was not good, I'm afraid. I remember stepping up to the counter where she worked to ask her to make a wire transfer. She refused, saying, "I'm not your personal secretary." I told her that I was a vice president of the firm and requested again that she do the wire transfer. Once again, she refused, telling me that if I wanted her to do the wire transfer, then I had to get the president of the company to approve it. Finally, after I got the president's okay, the wire transfer was completed. After that less-than-cordial encounter, you could say that she and I both noticed each other in the halls and offices of the brokerage firm as the months went by. Eventually, we became very good friends, fell in love, and married a year or so later.

By this time, it was the mid-1980s. There was a takeover at our brokerage firm, which resulted in the firm's changing from its independent contractor status to employee status. There was also a management change, and I was out of a job. I was unemployed, and my new wife was now pregnant. No worries, I did what any caring, loving, and intelligent husband would do: I borrowed $5,000 from my in-laws and started trading—specifically the S&P. The confluence of factors in my personal and professional life helped me to get very motivated and focus intensely.

A "STUDENT" OF THE MARKET

The book that started me on the right track of trading was *Technical Analysis of Stock Trends* by Robert D. Edwards and John Magee, which was first published in 1948. I practically memorized the book from cover to cover, and it gave me the foundation for a good understanding of how the market was supposed to work. I used the techniques in the book to trade commodities. I traded commodities for a whole year and managed *not* to lose the original $5,000 investment. This was quite an accomplishment in that I was still learning and somewhat a novice on this fast-track trading of commodities. This was the steepest learning curve in technical analysis I have encountered in my life to date and a crash course in trading survival. I was not working at this time, and my wife was carrying the load. Bills were running up and we had our baby daughter, Heather, to take care of. I went back to work as a stockbroker to help pay the bills.

By now it was 1988, the bills were paid, and, yes, I did pay back the loan to my loving in-laws. I was still hard at it, studying the markets. In the late 1980s, most indicators were hooked to price alone, such as moving average convergence/divergence (MACD), moving averages (MAs) of price, Elliott Wave or price wave analysis, relative strength index (RSI), stochastic oscillator, and so forth, all of which were price-based indicators. I studied all these methods in detail, but they did not give me a consistent, winning track record. In fact, I was using so many price-based indicators at one time that half would be saying one thing and the other half would be contradicting them.

This led me to a very important realization, which would become vital in the rest of my career as a trader and market analyst. I realized that price alone was not the only important factor in determining price direction. My first attempt to quantify price direction was with the New York Stock Exchange (NYSE) tick index, which compares the difference between the number of issues with the last trade higher (an uptick) from the previous price and the issues with the last trade lower (a downtick) from the previous price. This method was for short-term trading and worked well. By using the tick index method, in 1988 I placed fourth nationally in the United States Trading Championship in the option division.

Here's how the tick index method worked. Let's say exchange "Z" has 1,000 issues trading on an uptick and 500 issues trading on a downtick. The tick index would read "+1000 − 500 = +500." I used the tick index as an "exhaustion" indicator: When there were lots of high uptick index readings in a short time frame, then the NYSE was near a high; the opposite would occur when the market was near a low. What the tick index readings showed me was how hard the market was pushing in a direction at a particular time. When everyone was pushing through the door at the same time (high uptick reading), then the market was near a high. When everyone was trying to get out the door at the same time (high downtick readings), the market was near a low.

I measured extreme uptick readings from one high to another to look for lower uptick readings on the second high, indicating a negative divergence. This condition showed that the energy on the second high was less and that the market should reverse, which it usually did. Finding lows with the downtick readings worked the same way. I would look for high downtick readings from which the market would bounce, and then look for that low to be tested in the future. If the second downtick reading was less on the test of the previous low, then a bullish divergence would be created and the market should bounce. I became good at this trading method and started an option market letter called *The Ord Oracle* in 1990, using the tick index readings as my main indicator. (I also wrote three articles on the NYSE tick index for *Technical Analysis of Stocks & Commodities* magazine in 1991, 1992 and 1996.) The tick index readings gave me a good indication of where the market was on a short-term basis, but did not give me a good sense of the bigger trend.

Changes were also happening in the Ord household. In 1989, we bought 25 acres outside of Lincoln, Nebraska, with the plan to build our home there someday in the future. When I started *The Ord Oracle* market letter in 1990, I was operating out of our apartment in Colorado, faxing the reports after the close of the market each day. I also had a 900 number for customers to call for updates intraday. This was before the widespread use of the Internet. The world of information dissemination had not yet gone through its online explosion, although it was closer than I could have ever imagined in those days.

My market analysis was also continuing to evolve. Steve Nison's book, *Japanese Candlestick Charting Techniques*, was published in 1991, which I totally absorbed. The book identifies one- and two-day bullish and bearish patterns. I began combining my tick methods with candlestick charting and saw my win ratio improve. For sell signals, I used the tick index negative divergence on the retest of the second high with a bearish candlestick pattern. For bottoms, I looked for a positive divergence on the tick index on the retest of the first low that coincided with a bullish candlestick pattern, generating a buy signal.

AN INCOMPLETE PICTURE

What I discovered at this time in my journey into technical analysis is that price is affected by other factors, and that price alone is not a determining gauge of where prices are heading. Through my subscribers to *The Ord*

Oracle report, I received much information on new trading ideas that they had read in books, as well as some of their own techniques—some good, and some not so good. The more I studied, the more I was convinced that something was missing in my technical analysis, but I didn't know what it was. I could identify the short-term picture fairly well but the bigger picture was still unclear. It was as if I didn't have the entire picture of the market to make a complete analysis.

In 1993, we moved to Lincoln, Nebraska, and lived in a two-bedroom apartment for several months while our house was being built. We set up one bedroom as my office with one chair and a desk, and the other bedroom was our daughter's room with just her bed. Dawn and I slept on a mattress on the floor in the living room, where we also had a small, 13-inch television set. We had only sparse furnishings because we didn't want to move everything in and then have to move it all out again in a few months. It worked well for all of us. We hadn't made friends yet in our new town, so we had to rely on each other. My mother lived in a town 50 miles away, and we became close to her again.

The Ord Oracle report was going forward and we could see where life was heading, and we were excited about it. Then, in late 1993, we moved into our new home—with chairs and tables and real silverware and plates. Our new home was built in the middle of a field on 25 acres. Nothing else was around: no trees, not even bushes—nothing but land. I marked off about five acres that would become our lawn and rented the rest to a farmer. Over the next couple of years, I planted nearly 300 trees for a windbreak and put in a lawn and added a barn. We are still adding to this landscape, which has become a hobby of mine. When we built this home, we put in an eight-foot satellite receiver for stock quotes. In the mid-1990s, the Internet was starting to come on strong. My office probably had just as much market information as any brokerage office. I was still a broker at that time, although *The Ord Oracle* report was taking more time and producing higher earnings than the business of being a broker, but I kept both going into the mid-1990s.

UNDERSTANDING MARKET TIME FRAMES

At this time, I really started to understand the time frames of the market. I began to see that the bigger time frames ruled the smaller time frames, and that in order to have successful short-term trades, the larger time frame has to be in your favor. As I understood why the bigger picture of the market was so important, I also figured out why my trading method worked well in the first half of the year and not the second half, or vice versa. Simply put, when the market was going with my trading method,

I had good success, and when the market was going against my trading method, I did not do so well. As any trader will tell you, when the market beats you over the head with losses, you tend to learn from your mistakes. My big lesson: Before taking a trade, I had to make sure I was trading in the direction of the market. (This technique will be covered in detail in subsequent chapters.)

In the late 1990s, I continued to use and hone the tick index methods and was doing quite well with them. In 1998, I identified the October bottom by using the tick index method and recommended calls options on the market at that time to my subscribers to *The Ord Oracle* report. Some of these options appreciated over 400 percent in a couple of months. People started to take notice of my technical analysis abilities, and *The Ord Oracle* report circulation grew. In 1999, I was ranked third nationally by *Timer Digest* in trading the S&P 500. Since then, I have been frequently in the top 10 for trading the S&P 500 and the gold market to date.

"DISCOVERING" WYCKOFF

For any trader, lifelong learning is a must. No matter how well one does in the market, there is still much to learn and room to improve. In the late 1990s, one of my older subscribers to *The Ord Oracle* introduced me to a 1930s trading method developed by Richard Wyckoff, who was known for his studies of price and volume. This customer had a real handle on the market, more so than I did in those days. He told me that I had a very good and sound approach to the market, but in order to reach financial independence I needed to know how to use volume in my technical analysis. He explained that I could use Wyckoff's price and volume methods as the centerpiece, and then apply my technical analysis around that.

On his recommendation, I took a course in Wyckoff's methods. It took me more than a year to learn what Wyckoff was trying to convey in his market studies and to learn the methods that had made him famous and successful as a trader and investor back in the 1930s. After I understood how price and volume affect each other, a whole new view of the market came to light. It was 2001: a critical time in the market, with the bursting of the Nasdaq bubble and the market in a deep correction. With my understanding of price and volume, how the market functioned began to really make sense to me.

PRICE AND VOLUME RELATIONSHIPS

Before I understood price and volume relationships, I had endured many emotional days and sleepless nights, worrying about the positions I had in play and not being sure if they were correctly aligned. Although I was usually correct in my market calls, I felt my confidence was lacking in my signals sometimes. Price and volume analysis gave me extra concrete evidence and, therefore, more confidence in my signals. An extra plus was that price and volume analysis could be applied to any time frame—even one-minute charts. The rules did not change from one time frame to the next.

However, as I stated earlier in the chapter, the longer time frames rule over the shorter time frames. Thus, in order to trade successfully, you need to be sure that your trades are aligned with the longer-term trend in the market—even for a short-term trade. This will increase your chance of trading profitably.

I modified, simplified, and, in some cases, created new volume methods, and also updated some of the rules that Wyckoff put forth in his study materials that dated back to the 1930s. Some of the new volume rules I developed have never been revealed before, but once you see how they work on stocks, indexes, or anything that has volume, I believe you will trade with new confidence as you will know that you are trading in the direction of strength.

The tick index methods I developed to trade the markets in the late 1980s really jump-started my career in technical analysis and helped me become a successful short-term trader. The price and volume methods of Wyckoff established me as a successful trader and investor. To me, it really did not make sense to have all the technical tools set up with price only; it seemed too risky. Once I understood how price and volume worked together, then the function of price could be viewed through the forces of supply and demand. The reason a stock was trading at a certain level was that supply-and-demand pressures put it there. Think of it this way: *Supply* is another word for sellers—meaning, people sell their shares, which creates volume. *Demand* is another word for buyers, and when people buy shares, it also means volume. It is fundamental economics at work: If there is more demand than supply, the price is pushed higher, and if there is more supply than demand, then price is pushed lower. Supply and demand pressures push prices. The NYSE tick readings I had been using earlier had similar characteristics to volume, so for me it was an easy transition from tick analysis to volume analysis. Although there are many books out there on technical analysis, few emphasize the importance of volume analysis, so a lot of traders and investors don't know how to use volume correctly.

MY TRADING METHODOLOGY

The methods I discuss in this book use price and volume methodology, which are common in trading. There are no magic formulas or secret techniques. What makes this highly effective for me and of interest to other traders is that I have developed them to the point of precision. In this book, I will give examples of the software I have developed that show visually which way volume is pushing and, in turn, indicate where a stock is likely heading.

In the chapters to come, I will explain how I use volume analysis in ways that I have found to work very well. For example, I found that the "top-down" approach to investing works well for me. Using the top-down approach, first you determine the direction of the market (whether NYSE, Nasdaq, or S&P 500), and trade that direction in the issues that you select. If the market is in a bullish trend, then take only long positions; and in a bearish trend, take only short positions.

Second, if the market is in a bullish trend, then you must also be in one of the most bullish sectors. (Again, the opposite works for a bearish trend.) Third, you attempt to buy the most bullish stocks in the most bullish sectors. Picking the direction of the market and choosing the best sector to be in and the best stocks in the best sector will be covered in the coming chapters.

Although it might seem to be a daunting task to pick the direction of the market, I have discovered several techniques to help you, which I will explain in the book. I also have a technique for picking the best sectors that has worked well over the years. Now think about how this approach will help your profitability. If you have the market right and you have the sector right, it would be hard to lose money in a stock if both the market and sector are pulling up your stock. By following the top-down approach, you are not in the market all the time if you are trading only the long side. You trade the long side only when the market is in a bullish trend and the sector is in a bullish trend. If markets are in a downtrend, then you are waiting on the sideline until the market turns bullish. You are trading only when the odds are in your favor, and that is when the market and the sector are in your favor.

My earlier years in trading and my technical analysis journey were downright frightening at times. I stumbled and fell, got up, and persevered. There was a whole array of factors that I discovered in real-time trading that came from the hard knocks I took along the way. For me, that was the only way I could have learned. If my journey had been easier, I probably would have not become the disciplined technical analysis trader that I am today.

My road to trading successfully was filled with potholes. If that's been your experience, too, then don't despair. Twenty-five years later, I can tell you that the journey has been well worth it. My journey helped me to discover and explore what worked for me, which I will share in detail. And as the saying goes, it is not the destination, but the journey in life that is so rewarding. My journey continues in my technical analysis study, looking for more concrete ways to determine and confirm market direction. Thank you for sharing this leg of the journey with me.

CHAPTER 2

Overview of My Method

To make money consistently as a trader, it's essential to know the overall direction of the market in the longer-term time frames. It would be difficult to make money with a long position in a stock if the overall market were heading down. The opposite would be true with a short position in a stock if the market were heading higher.

In the investment world, as they say, "a rising tide lifts all boats." That means that most stocks will follow a rising trend (like having the "wind at your back," if you will). In order to take advantage of these market axioms, what works best for me is to take trades in the direction of the market. To do that, I first determine the market's direction, and then I find the best sectors to be in, and after that I pick one of the best stocks in a best sector.

But before we get into market direction, sector analysis, and stock analysis, we must start with time frames.

TIME FRAMES AND TRADING

It seems that the younger trading crowd prefers the short-term time frames, and, as they age, their preferred time frame extends. I know I was that way. When I was a young trader, I figured that if a stock moved up or down a point in one day, then I could catch that move by trading intraday. That would enable me to make a lot of money in a very short period of time.

I added on to that idea by trading options, which allowed me to leverage my position even more than simply trading stock. My thinking at the time was that by trading options, which gave me the advantage of leverage, and using a short-term time frame, I'd be rich in no time! Or so I thought.

Although I don't want to discourage anyone from going in that direction, I found that it was a difficult undertaking for me. For many people, decision making is one of the most challenging things to do. Trading an intraday time frame requires many difficult decisions to be made several times a day—and with each one there are financial consequences. Given these pressures, it won't take long for traders to evaluate what trading time frame they're best suited to handle.

If the speed and intensity of intraday trading activity is not for you, take heart: There is a way to achieve financial trading success without all the frustration of rapid decision making. I have found that the longer time frames of three to six months, along with taking a "top-down approach," alleviates a lot of the frustration of trading and provide greater clarity (and therefore more confidence) in making trades.

TAKING A TOP-DOWN APPROACH

Using the top-down approach, you begin by looking at the whole market first, and then determine in which direction the market is going using a three- to six-month time frame. Personally, I prefer to trade from the long side. Thus, if the market is in a downtrend I will stay on the sidelines until it turns around. If the whole market is in an uptrend, I will then undertake sector analysis to determine the most bullish sectors to be in. Once I have identified the most bullish sectors, I will pick the most bullish stocks in that sector.

This is the essence of the three-step top-down approach, moving from the trend of the market in the bigger picture of the longer time frame, and then looking at sectors and, after that, particular stocks.

Consider the merits of the top-down approach for a moment. Let's say you have correctly pegged the direction of the market, and it is rallying. In addition, you've successfully identified one of the best sectors, and it is also rallying. Plus, you have picked a strong stock in one of the best sectors. It would be difficult for your stock not to go up. Look at all the factors favoring your trade. The general market trend is pulling up your stock, and the sector is also adding to the upward momentum. You have put the odds decidedly in your favor.

When the overall market and the sector you have picked are both aligned in your favor, that is the only time to put your money to work in the market. If you share my preference to trade from the long side, when the market or the sector turns bearish, you would head back to the sidelines. This method requires patience, but it has the potential to pay big rewards.

I have always been a visual person. For me, the saying, "A picture is worth a thousand words," holds very true. In the next several pages, I will show you examples of charts that show visually how the top-down approach works. In subsequent chapters, I will explain in detail how signals are generated for the market, sectors, and stocks.

The markets I follow closely for signal generation are the Standard & Poor's (S&P) 500 Index, Nasdaq, and the gold indexes of "Capped Gold Index ($SPTGD) and "Market Vectors Gold Miners" (GDX). I also follow the "Gold and Silver Index–Philadelphia" ($XAU), but volume for this index is not readily available, and volume plays a very important role in determining the strength of a particular issue. (This concept will be covered later in detail.) However, both the Capped Gold Index and Market Vectors Gold Miners show volume, which is the main reason I track these indexes for signals in the gold sector.

At this point, let's quickly review the three steps of the top-down approach:

1. Find the direction of the overall market.
2. Select the best sectors.
3. Find the strongest stocks in the best sector.

Evaluating Breadth, Volume, and Momentum

First, we are going to look briefly at the market as a whole and pick out highs and lows. I will go into this in detail later, but the most important considerations in picking highs and lows in the market are breadth, volume, and momentum.

Breadth measures the number of issues in an index that is advancing and the number that is declining. When someone says that the market has "bad breadth," this does not mean halitosis. Rather, it means that the market has more declining issues than advancing issues, which is a bearish scenario for the market.

In a healthy market, most of the stocks will be advancing, and stock leadership will be broad based. Tops are found in the market when stock leadership narrows, and only a few stocks carry the rally forward. The top comes when these last few stocks make their highs.

Breadth Analysis For breadth analysis, I use the McClellan Oscillator and Summation Index developed by Sherman and Marion McClellan back in the 1960s. The McClellan Oscillator and Summation Index have stood the test of time and are among the best indicators for determining breadth.

The formula for the McClellan Oscillator is fairly complex. To keep it short and simple, it is basically the result of subtracting a 39-day exponential average of advances minus declines (5 percent index) from a 19-day exponential average (10 percent index). The McClellan Summation Index is derived by adding together the previous day's McClellan Summation Index and the current day's McClellan Oscillator. (To learn more about the McClellan Oscillator and Summation Index, you can write to: McClellan Financial Publication, Inc., P.O. Box 39779, Lakewood, WA 98439-0779.)

I use the McClellan Oscillator and Summation Index as a breadth indicator of the New York Stock Exchange (NYSE) because it gives a good indication of where the market is at any given time. I prefer to use the Summation Index of the NYSE, instead of the S&P 500, because the Summation Index for the NYSE has smoother runs from high to low and low to high, and also has less volatility. Therefore, it produces clearer signals.

The Summation Index acts like an oscillator that vacillates between overbought to oversold levels. As I've seen over the past three years, when the Summation Index for the NYSE is above +3,500, then the market is overbought and near a high. Further, when the NYSE Summation Index is below −500, then the market is oversold and near a low. In the years to come, the overbought and oversold levels may change, but these variations should be gradual, as they were in the past, allowing us to make adjustments.

Figure 2.1 dates back to the beginning of 2004, showing four times when the Summation Index for the NYSE dipped below −500. In each case, the NYSE was near a low.

A buy signal is triggered when the Summation Index for the NYSE trades below −500 and then closes above −500. A close above −500 indicates a buy for the NYSE. This trading method did a good job of identifying the significant lows over the past several years. All of the buy signals determined by this method have lasted several months, giving traders ample time to make money on the long side because the odds were in their favor.

Figure 2.2 shows the Summation Index for the NYSE trading above +3,500 five times. A "shot over the bow" warning signal indicates a top is approaching when the Summation Index for the NYSE rallies above +3,500 and then closes below the +3,500 level. A close below +3,500 indicates "the shot over the bow" for the NYSE. Tops in markets take longer to develop than bottoms, and take more study to identify. However, take heart that there are clues and ways to find tops in markets successfully. (The detailed method using the McClellan Summation Index will be covered in Chapter 6.)

In early 2007, a "shot over the bow" signal was triggered twice for the NYSE with the Summation Index closing below the +3,500 level. The

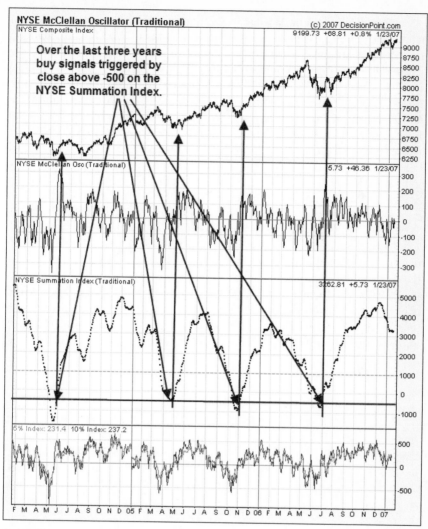

FIGURE 2.1   McClellan Oscillator for NYSE Shows Buy Signals Generated by a Close above −500 Level
Source: Chart courtesy of DecisionPoint.com.

"shot over the bow" was not a sell signal, but rather a warning that a top was approaching and traders should take appropriate steps in preparing their accounts for the pending top. Other signals were triggered using this method in January 2005, August 2005, February 2006, January 2007, and February 2007. (The complete sell signal method by the McClellan Oscillator will be covered in Chapter 6. An overview is presented in this chapter.)

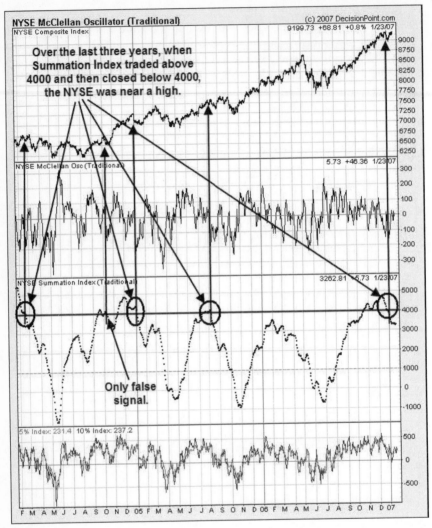

FIGURE 2.2   McClellan Oscillator for NYSE Shows "Shot over the Bow" Signals Triggered by a Close below 13,500 Level
Source: Chart courtesy of DecisionPoint.com.

In October 2004, a "shot over the bow" was triggered when the Summation Index went above +3,500 and then closed below that level. The market and the Summation Index did head lower for a couple of weeks before both reversed and headed higher, breaking to new highs. (This failed signal will be covered in Chapter 6, along with an explanation of what to do in case a signal is rejuvenated.)

Volume Analysis　I'm a big fan of volume. In any market, two things need to be present: price and, equally important, volume at that price. Price, of course, shows the levels at which an instrument is bought and sold. The activity at each price level creates volume. The buyer of an issue must be paired up with a seller of the same issue at an agreed-upon price for that moment in time. Simply put, volume pushes price. If there is more demand (more buyers) for an issue, then prices rise. If there is more supply (more sellers), then prices fall.

It's clear that volume is vitally important to any study of the market. In fact, I believe that volume analysis is one of the most important studies that should be undertaken. Too few traders, however, know how to use volume correctly in their analyses.

Figure 2.3 is a weekly chart of Bema Gold Corporation (symbol: BGO). Here, BGO provides a good, visual example of supply and demand. You can see how prices increase as volume expands and prices decline as volume contracts. If volume is increasing as price is advancing, and

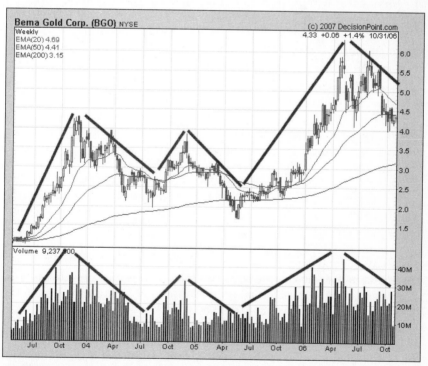

FIGURE 2.3　　Bema Gold Chart Shows, in a Bullish Trend, Volume Increases as Prices Rise and Volume Decreases as Prices Decline
Source: Chart courtesy of DecisionPoint.com.

price is decreasing as volume is contracting, then the bullish trend should continue. The reason: When prices go up, the sellers are more willing to meet buyers at those higher levels and volume increases. When prices go down, however, sellers head to the sidelines, believing they'll be able to sell at higher prices later on. This activity shows a bullish undertone.

If volume increases on the downward "legs" (segments of market activity or movements), and contracts on the upward legs, then the bullish trend has turned into a bearish one. What's happening is that, in order to attract buyers, prices have to go lower. When prices head higher, the buyers go to the sidelines, believing that they'll be able to buy at lower prices later on. This creates a bearish undertone.

With this understanding, you can see that stocks trend in the direction of the highest volume. Stocks correct or consolidate on lighter volume. By measuring the volume of an issue between the swings higher and lower, and comparing that volume to previous swing intervals, traders can "see" the force of a particular move developing in a stock. (A "swing" is a high or low in an issue at which the price trend changes direction.)

Here are two rules to help traders understand the interpretation of volume comparisons:

1. In an uptrend, a stock should have higher volume on the rally phase than during the correction phase.
2. In a downtrend, a stock should have higher volume on the declining phase than during the up-correction phase.

Figure 2.4 is a chart of BGO that also shows the average daily volume between the swings. I have nicknamed this average daily volume Ord-Volume, since it is the basis of my volume analysis in trading. By studying the Ord-Volume, as depicted in this chart, you can see how volume pushes price. (In the next chapter, I will explain why average daily volume is the way to measure strength in a move rather than looking at the total volume between the swings.)

I think of Ord-Volume as the "energy" or force behind a move. The greater the energy, the stronger the conviction of the players in the market. In Figure 2.4 you can see, going into the August 2004 low, Ord-Volume evaporated. This suggested that there was no more energy pushing to the downside. The market was sold out and a bottom was near.

On the next leg up, Ord-Volume increased by 65 percent, showing that energy had increased to the upside compared to the previous leg down. This confirmed a low was made. On the next leg down from the December 2004 high, Ord-Volume came in 16 percent less than in the previous leg up, showing that there was more force to the upside, and the trend remained bullish.

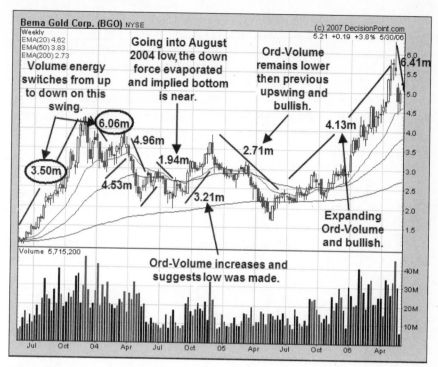

FIGURE 2.4   Comparison of Volume between Swings—Known as "Ord-Volume"
Source: Chart courtesy of DecisionPoint.com.

The next up leg from the May 2005 low was a major impulse wave. Ord-Volume expanded and confirmed the up leg. Now, notice what happened at the May 2006 time frame. Ord-volume switched from up to down. This change in energy suggested that a top was made—which was similar to how the top was made at the November 2003 high. This is the way that volume works with price. To trade successfully, a trader must know which way volume is pushing. In the next chapter, I will explain how signals are generated with volume analysis.

Momentum Analysis   A momentum indicator smoothes out price fluctuations of an issue so it is easier to see what direction price is moving. When a momentum indicator is rising on an issue, then that issue is in an uptrend, and when the indicator is decline, the issue is in a downtrend. There are numerous momentum indicators that can be used by traders. The indicator I like and use the most is the Price Momentum Oscillator (PMO) developed by Carl Swenlin, president of www.decisionpoint.com, a web site for technical analysis traders.

PMO is a proprietary indicator. However, it is based on a rate-of-change calculation, which is exponentially smoothed. PMO works and looks similar to the moving average convergence/divergence (MACD) momentum oscillator developed by Gerald Appel. MACD is a good substitute if you don't have access to the PMO indicator.

Both PMO and MACD are useful for identifying the larger trend of an issue. I prefer the longer time frame of three to six months, and use the weekly PMO to identify signals in this time frame. The weekly PMO also lines up well with the McClellan Summation Index and helps to confirm or deny the bullish or bearish case of the underlying index.

Bullish and bearish crossovers of the 10-day exponential moving average generate buy and sell signals for the PMO. Figure 2.5 shows the weekly Nasdaq Composite dating back to late 2001. When the 10-day exponential moving average crosses over the PMO, a sell signal is triggered.

In Figure 2.5, you can see the sell signals going back to early 2002 that were triggered by the bearish crossover of the weekly PMO. Sometimes,

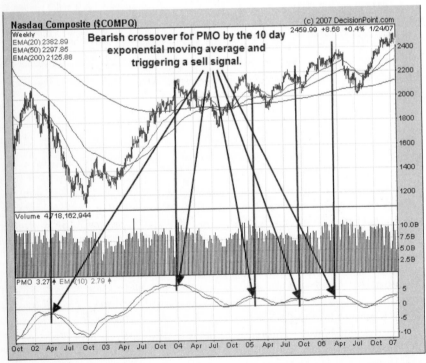

FIGURE 2.5   Nasdaq Composite Chart Shows Sell Signals Triggered by Bearish Crossovers for the PMO
Source: Chart courtesy of DecisionPoint.com.

the bearish PMO signal is triggered a little early or a little late, but overall it does a fine job of picking the turns. Notice most bearish signals that were triggered on the bearish crossover for the weekly PMO lasted several months.

Figure 2.6 shows the weekly Nasdaq Composite going back to late 2001. Note the bullish crossover of the 10-day exponential moving average of the weekly PMO that triggered buy signals.

The buy signals triggered on the weekly PMO lasted several months, giving a trader ample time to make money on the long side. Had you been trading during this time with this methodology, you would have been long when the buy signal was triggered by the bullish PMO crossover. The odds of making money in stocks and/or indexes would have been in your favor because the overall market was moving upward.

PMO and MACD indicators also can be used when the market is overbought and oversold. Figure 2.7 is a weekly NYSE chart, showing weekly MACD and PMO oscillators. Since 2003, intermediate-term tops form on

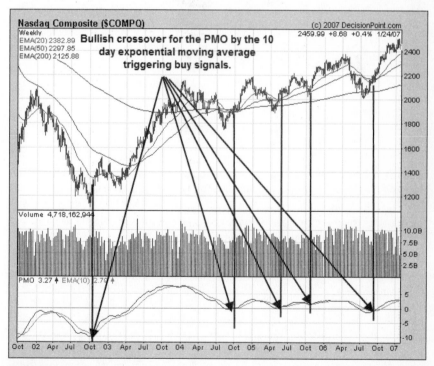

FIGURE 2.6   Nasdaq Composite Chart Shows Buy Signals Triggered by Bullish Crossovers for the PMO
Source: Chart courtesy of DecisionPoint.com.

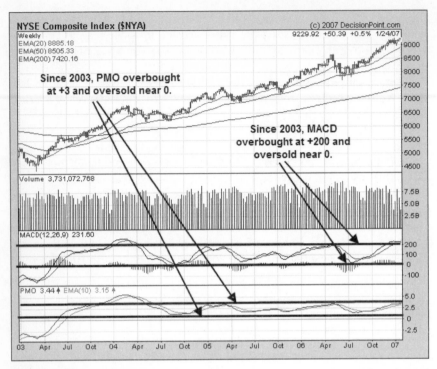

FIGURE 2.7   NYSE Chart Depicts Oversold and Overbought Levels Indicated by PMO and MACD
Source: Chart courtesy of DecisionPoint.com.

the NYSE when the MACD is near +200 and the PMO is near +3. Bottoms for the NYSE are indicated when the MACD and the PMO are near 0.

The chart in Figure 2.7 was created in January 2007. At that time, notice that the weekly MACD was at +200 and weekly PMO was at +3, implying that NYSE was overbought.

The MACD and PMO also help to identify bull and bear markets. Figure 2.8 shows the NYSE weekly chart with weekly MACD and PMO indicators. When MACD and PMO stay below the "0" line, a bearish market is in progress. When MACD and PMO stay above the "0" line, it is a bull market.

Notice in early 2001, the weekly MACD and weekly PMO passed through the "0" line, signaling a bearish market had begun. These indicators were below the "0" line for the duration of the bear market. MACD and PMO crossed above the "0" line in 2003, signaling the start of a bull market. The MACD and PMO, in general, stayed above the "0" line from 2003 to present, implying a bull market in force.

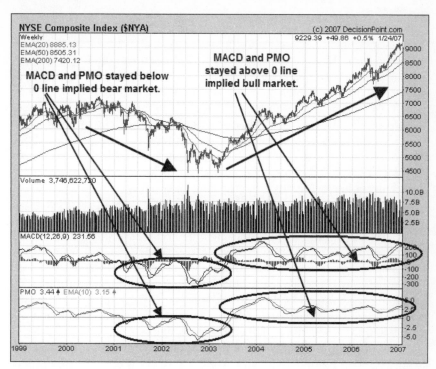

FIGURE 2.8 NYSE Chart Shows Bullish and Bearish Market Readings Determined by MACD and PMO
Source: Chart courtesy of DecisionPoint.com.

In early 2007, the MACD and PMO were still above "0," indicating that the bull market was still alive. However, the overbought conditions of +200 on the MACD and +3 on PMO suggested that a pullback was possible for the shorter term. Also recall from the section on the McClellan Oscillator on the NYSE, the Summation Index also showed a bearish "shot over the bow" setup twice, which reinforced the idea that a pullback was likely starting in early 2007.

The weekly signals of MACD and PMO do lag in timing, but still help to show where the markets are at any given time, indicating whether a bull or bear market is present.

At this point, we have a good, foundational understanding of how breadth, volume, and momentum affect the markets, and how bullish and bearish signals are generated. Next, we move to finding the best sector to be in.

Understanding Sector Analysis

First, let's define what we mean by sector. It is a group of stocks in the same industry. Examples of sectors include semiconductors, banking, and so forth. With that understanding, let's consider when we move to sector analysis. As I explained, my trading methodology favors the long side. We'll start with the bottom that formed in June 2006 on the NYSE. (A complete analysis of how that low was identified will be given in Chapter 3.) For now, to help simplify matters, assume that we have identified the bottom at the June 2006 low, and we are now bullish based on the view for the next three to six months. With this long-term view, we have a chance to trade profitability from the long side.

With the market in a bullish mode, our goal is to find the stocks that will appreciate the most, giving us the "biggest bang for the buck," so to speak. This is the most opportune time to be bullish, since most stocks are coming off a low point and are relatively cheap. (If you want to buy stocks on margin, I believe this is the only time it would be safe to do so.)

So how do you pick stocks that are the best positioned to appreciate the most for the next three to six months? First of all, the initial step is not to pick the stock. Rather, you find the strongest sector within the overall market. Then you pick the best stock in that sector.

This two-step process will get you closer to your goal of picking the strongest stock more quickly and easily. There are thousands upon thousands of stocks in the market, and picking the one that is likely to appreciate the most is a monumental task. However, there are only 36 or so sectors (depending on how the sectors are broken down). This is a much easier number to deal with.

Sector Strength   Grouping stocks into sectors and then running scans to find the strongest sectors saves both time and energy. Using the June 2006 scenario, we already know the time is right because, looking at the big picture and a long-term time frame, we know the market has made a bottom. Now the time is right to find the best sector and the best stock within that sector.

Sector strength can be identified by studying what happens to that sector in a declining NYSE market. Strong sectors will drop less on a percentage basis compared with weak sectors; therefore, the sectors that hold up the best during a decline should perform the best when the next rally phase begins. The rationale is a sector that doesn't go down as much in a bear market should really fly when the overall market rallies.

The rule is that sector strength is identified by price strength in an overall market decline. This is analogous to the way an investor may pick one stock over another on a retracement of a previous up leg. One stock pulls back 50 percent of its previous up leg. Another stock only pulls back 38 percent of its previous up leg. The stock that pulled back the least on a percentage basis is the stronger stock. Identifying sector strength works the same way.

Figure 2.9 shows the S&P 500 Large Cap Index ($SPX). A strong rally in the S&P started in June 2006 and lasted into December 2006, amounting to nearly 200 points or a 16 percent gain.

Figure 2.10 is a sector comparison chart (found on www.stockcharts .com). It depicts what John Murphy, chief technical analyst of StockCharts .com, likes to compare in economic cycles. The nine sectors of banks, gold and silver, semiconductors, oil services, pharmaceuticals, S&P 500 retail, Internet, biotech, and brokers provide a good cross-section of the economy.

By charting these sectors, displaying one on top of another graphically, we can see which sectors hold up the best going into a market bottom. The sectors that went down the least in these market conditions should also

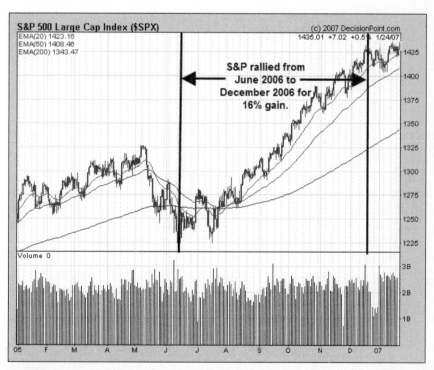

FIGURE 2.9   Chart of S&P 500 Large Cap Index Shows Rally from June 2006 to December 2006
Source: Chart courtesy of DecisionPoint.com.

Major US Markets PerfChart

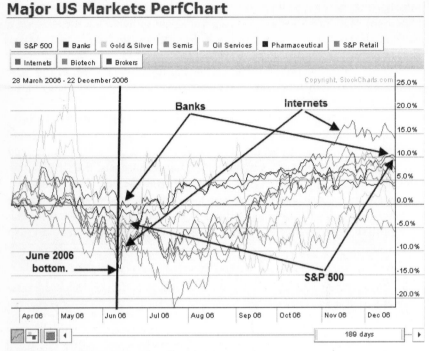

FIGURE 2.10   Major Market Performance Chart Compares Strengths of Various Sectors
Source: Chart courtesy of StockCharts.com.

be the ones that perform the best during the next market rally. In other words, the sectors that went down the least in a down market should go up the most in an up market.

Notice in Figure 2.10 that the sector "banks" held up the best at the June 2006 bottom. In mid-December 2006, bank stocks as a group were up nearly 12.5 percent. However, compare the performance of the banks with the S&P. The S&P came from a couple of percentage points below the banks at the June 2006 low, and ended up at near the same level as the banks as of December 2006. That performance comparison shows why the S&P performed a little better than the banks.

The sector that performed the best in this time frame was the Internet stocks. The Internets started from a much lower low and showed weakness going into the June 2006 low compared to the S&P and the banks. However, the Internets rallied strongly and outperformed all markets. The reason why is not clear. However, this sector analysis method certainly did a decent job of picking one of the best sectors in terms of performance from the June 2006 low.

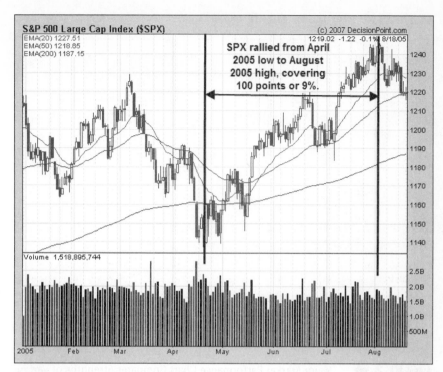

FIGURE 2.11 S&P 50 Large Cap Index Shows Rally from April 2005 Low to August 2005 High
Source: Chart courtesy of DecisionPoint.com.

Figure 2.11 shows another time frame—low to high—from April 2005 to August 2005. The S&P 500 covered 100 points in that time frame, or a gain of about 9 percent.

Going into the April 2005 bottom, as Figure 2.12 depicts, the two strongest sectors that held up the best were oil services and pharmaceuticals. Oil services did the best by appreciating 28 percent, while pharmaceuticals did not do as well, breaking about even.

This example shows why sector analysis is very important. It's always wise to pick two or three sectors to invest in at the lows to spread the risk; otherwise, there is a chance that the one sector that you are in may not perform. In this example, you would have made money in oil services but broke even in pharmaceuticals.

Stock Selection

Stock selection is similar to picking sector strength. As explained in the previous section, the sector that holds up the best going into a low is

Major US Markets PerfChart

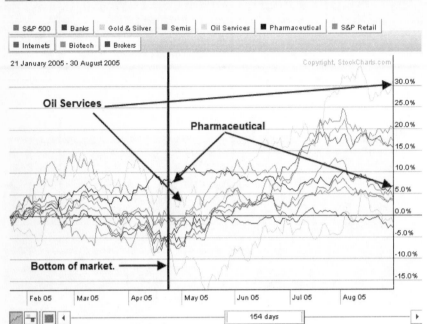

FIGURE 2.12   Major Market Performance Chart Shows Performance of Oil Services and Pharmaceuticals
Source: Chart courtesy of StockCharts.com.

one of the strongest sectors. This method also works well to pick strong stocks within a strong sector.

Here's an example: As noted earlier, the oil service sector was one of the strongest sectors at the April 2005 bottom. The stocks comprising this sector are: Transocean, Inc. (RIG), Cooper Cameron Corporation (CAM), Global Santa Fe Corporation (GSF), Baker Hughes, Inc. (BHI), Noble Drilling Corporation (NE), Tidewater, Inc. (TDW), Schlumberger Ltd. (SLB), Smith Intl, Inc. (SII), Nabors Industries, Inc. (NBR), and Halliburton Company (HAL).

Figure 2.13 shows a comparison chart (found on www.stockcharts. com) that allows us to pick 10 issues and compare them to each other to show which ones held up the best going into a low. (*Note:* If a sector had 20 issues, then this task would be done twice to compare all issues.)

Figure 2.13 shows that Halliburton and Cooper Cameron held up the best going into the April 2005 low. As of the next high in the market in August 2005 Halliburton was up 40 percent and Cooper Cameron had

PerfChart
(RIG,GSF,BHI,CAM,NE,TDW,SLB,SII,NBR,HAL)
Interactive Performance Comparison Chart

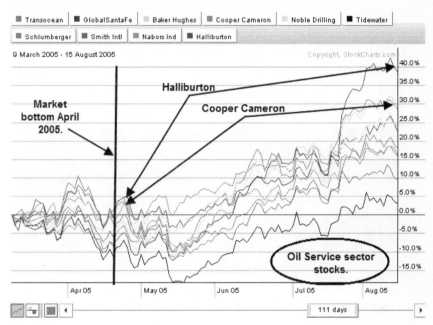

FIGURE 2.13 Chart Comparing Performance of Oil Service Sector Stocks
Source: Chart courtesy of StockCharts.com.

risen 30 percent. By comparison, the S&P was up 9 percent in this time frame. This shows what a powerful tool stock section is in a trader's technical toolkit.

Now let's take a look at the pharmaceutical sector, which also held up well going into the April 2005 low. However, as we saw earlier, it did not perform as well as oil services going into the August 2005 high. This underscores the importance of trading stocks from at least two top-performing sectors in order to spread the risk. The oil services was profitable. However, the pharmaceutical sector posted a 5 percent gain as of the August 2005 high, compared with the 30 percent increase in the oil services sector.

The stocks comprising the pharmaceutical sector are Schering Plough Corporation (SGP), Abbott Labs (ABT), Bristol Myers Squibb Company (BMY), Forest Labs. Inc. (FRX), King Pharmaceuticals Inc. (KG), Glaxo Wellcome PLC (GSK), Sanofi Aventis (SNY), Merck & Company, Inc. (MRK), Teva Pharma (TEVA), and Wyeth (WYE).

PerfChart
(SGP,ABT,FRX,KG,CSK,SNY,MRK,TEVA,WYE,BMY)
Interactive Performance Comparison Chart

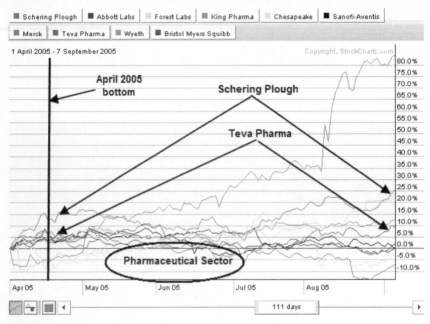

FIGURE 2.14   Chart Comparing Performance of Pharmaceutical-Sector Stocks
Source: Chart courtesy of StockCharts.com.

Figure 2.14 shows that Schering Plough and Teva Pharma held up the best among 10 stocks in the sector going into April 2005 low. The stocks were up about 15 percent and 5 percent, respectively, at the April 2005 low.

As of August 2005, Schering Plough was up 25 percent, netting a gain of 10 percent in that time frame, and Teva Pharma rose 10 percent for a net gain of 5 percent. Both stocks did make modest gains and were a profitable investment. But they did not have the performance of the oil-sector stocks. Again, this points to the necessity of picking more than one top-performing sector.

ALIGNING WITH THE MARKET

The top-down approach outlined in this chapter is a three-step process that determines the market direction first, focuses on the strongest sectors second, and then zeroes in on the strongest stocks in the strongest sectors. The purpose is to create greater alignment with the market, and to let the market carry your stock selections higher.

Investment novices think that investing is easy. We've all heard the stories of monkeys picking stocks by throwing darts at stock tables in the newspaper. If a monkey can do it, the novices tell themselves, then so can I! What the novices don't understand is that those monkeys don't have any outside influences to support or counter their dart throwing.

The rest of us, however, are bombarded with myriad influences. There are the financial television shows, web sites, blogs, and opinions touted by so-called experts, amateurs, and financial journalists alike—who sometimes end up being 180 degrees off the mark!

Information is one thing, but information overload is quite another. To cope, I rely on breadth, volume, and momentum analysis alone to give me an objective view of which way the market is moving. Breadth, volume, and momentum are the facts of the market, and they do not lie. Stay with the facts and you will increase your chances of having a rewarding investment career.

CHAPTER 3

Physics of Price and Volume Analysis

O f all the technical tools that I use to determine the direction of the market, the most reliable and accurate ones for making a forecast are price and volume. To better understand how volume works with price, substitute the word *energy* for the word *volume*. Now you can see what effect volume has on price. Volume energizes price; volume pushes price.

When there is no volume, price does not move; it is like a car that has run out of gas. When volume is added to price (just like when gas is put into the tank of the car), then price will move. Prices will move up or down depending on whether there are more buyers or sellers. With this understanding, you can see how volume is really a force of price propulsion. In that, it is like the study of physics.

Price can be accelerated in one direction or another with an increase in volume, just as the speed of a car increases when you step on the gas pedal. Strong rallies or sharp declines in the market are typically accompanied by high volume.

To see this force in action, look at Figure 3.1, which depicts a chart of Research in Motion Ltd. (RIMM). From its October 2000 high, RIMM started to fall on high volume, which provided good force (energy) to the downside.

As RIMM neared its low, volume contracted and there was less force in the market because there were fewer sellers. This foretold that a bottom was approaching. Then, in October 2002, volume began to pick up again and prices started to move. As Figure 3.1 also shows, with more buyers in the market, volume escalated and prices started to rise. Looking

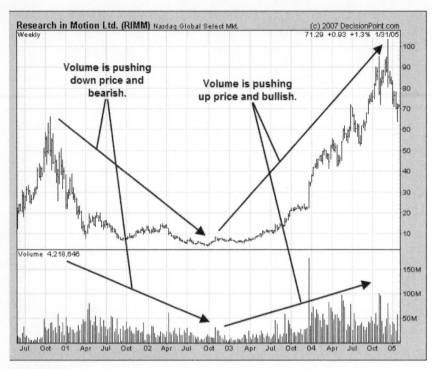

FIGURE 3.1   Volume Provides the Downward Energy to Push Down the Price
of Research in Motion (RIMM) during a Bearish Move
Source: Chart courtesy of DecisionPoint.com.

at the price and volume over this span of time, we can see that after
the bottom was in place, the volume force had switched from downward
to upward, and RIMM was now on an upswing. Price and volume
advanced together for the next two years, and the stock reached a high in
October 2004.

This information is nice to know and easy to see in hindsight. But
how can we use this knowledge to help us be successful in the market
real time? Let's start with what we know: Volume is energy that moves
prices. By studying this energy, we can forecast highs and lows in stocks
and indexes.

Before going further, we have to identify a few terms:

- **Swing:** A high or low where the price of a stock, index, or other issue
  changes direction.
- **Leg:** The distance between two swings.

To illustrate these two terms, let's look at a bar chart of the hypothetical stock "ABC." In Figure 3.2, you can see the volume of each rally leg up to a swing high, and then the volume of each bar in the decline leg. The number below each bar is the volume on that particular day.

The volume on rally legs and on decline legs can tell a great deal about which way a stock, index, or other issue is heading. In Figure 3.2, the stock "ABC" rallied for four days on volume of 2,000 per day, for a total of 8,000. It then declined for three days on volume of 2,000, 3,000, and 3,000, for a total of 8,000. Just based on this simple arithmetic, it would appear that the upward energy or force was equal to the downward energy. This is not, however, the correct way to measure force in a leg.

The correct way to measure the force in a leg is by using *average daily volume*. This will give you the correct reading in a rally leg or a decline leg. In this example, average daily volume on the rally is 2,000. The average daily volume on the decline is 2,667. This shows that the down leg had 667 more volume—or 33 percent more force (energy) to the downside. For a stock to have an uptrend, the rally legs need to have higher average volume than the decline legs.

I have coined the term *Ord-Volume* to describe average daily volume in a leg, which is part of my proprietary work on price and volume analysis. (I have also developed software that performs Ord-Volume studies on stocks and indices, which will be seen in examples later in this chapter.)

In Chapter 2, we examined a weekly chart of Bema Gold Corporation (BGO). Now, let's look at BGO with its average daily volume—or Ord-Volume—for each leg, showing which way the volume force is pushing

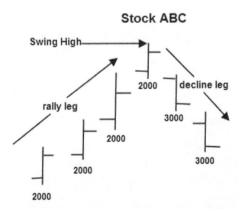

Stock ABC

FIGURE 3.2 Bar Chart of a Hypothetical Stock "ABC" Showing the Daily Volume during a Rally Leg to a Swing High and Then the Daily Volume of a Decline Leg

in each leg. Figure 3.3 depicts a weekly chart of BGO over a three-year period with its Ord-Volume displayed for each leg.

Figure 3.4 shows BGO in Ord-Volume format—a line chart that displays the average daily volume between the high and low swings. At the swings, price and volume are displayed. At the bottom of the chart is an exaggerated volume chart to better show visually volume changes. Although a simpler chart than the candlestick chart in Figure 3.3, Figure 3.4 displays the most relevant information to make financial decisions.

What we are most interested in is when and where a market changes direction. These points, or swings, are the areas at which to make a financial investment where risk is comparatively smaller and the potential gain is higher. For a bullish trend to continue, the up legs need to have more energy than the down leg, and vice versa for a bearish market.

Figure 3.5 also shows BGO in Ord-Volume format, with a major rally leg that began in July 2003 with average daily volume of 3.50 million.

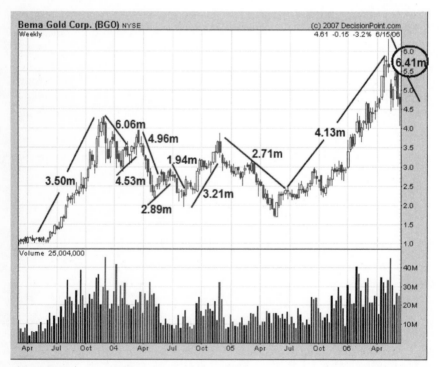

FIGURE 3.3   Ord-Volume Shows the Up and Down Force behind Each Move in Bema Gold (BGO)
Source: Chart courtesy of DecisionPoint.com.

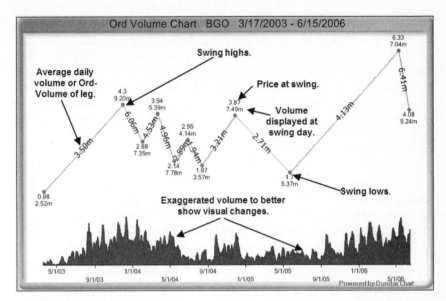

FIGURE 3.4 Average Daily Volume Shown in Ord-Volume Format for Bema Gold (BGO)

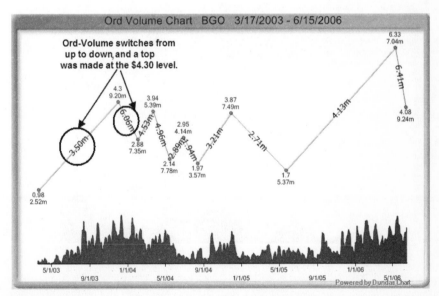

FIGURE 3.5 Ord-Volume Chart for Bema Gold (BGO) Showing a Shift in Energy from the Upside to the Downside

The rally lasted into December 2003 when a top was put in at $4.30 a share. In the decline leg Ord-Volume was 6.06 million—nearly double the amount of volume in the rally leg. This showed that energy had shifted from up to down, and confirmed the top at the $4.30 level. As interesting as that may be, it does not do us a whole lot of good after the fact. What's needed is a way of detecting changes in energy.

The Ord-Volume software that I use has a "zoom" feature, which increases or decreases the swing degrees. The lower the "zoom" setting, the smaller-degree swings that are revealed, and vice versa. In Figure 3.6, we examine BGO with "zoom" settings focusing on the period of time from October 15 through December 15, 2003, when the stock put in a high. (The zoom setting was 0.25 to show the smaller degree swings in that time frame. As you can see, these smaller-degree swings also have strong energy to the downside versus the upside.)

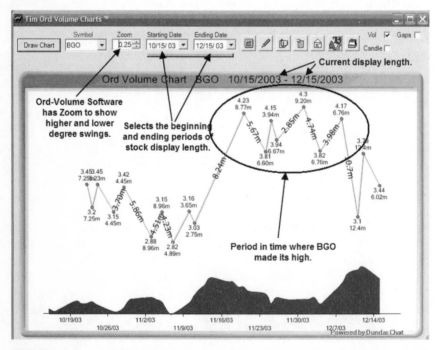

FIGURE 3.6   "Zoom" Setting on Ord-Volume Software Shows Smaller Degree Swings as Bema Gold (BGO) Put in a High

DETERMINING BUY AND SELL SIGNALS USING ORD-VOLUME

Before continuing, we need to look at how a buy and sell signals are triggered by the Ord-Volume method, and explain how a stronger or weaker signal is generated.

A sell signal is triggered when a stock hits a minor new high and the Ord-Volume on the current up leg shrinks by approximately 50 percent or greater compared with the Ord-Volume of the previous up leg or down leg; the stock then closes below the previous high. Both conditions determine the stock is in a weak position. This triggers the sell signal. Confirmation of a top is produced when Ord-Volume increases by 50 percent or more on the down leg after the top compared to the up leg going into the top.

Conversely, we know a bottom has been made—triggering a buy signal—when a stock hits a minor new low and Ord-Volume shrinks near 50 percent or greater against the previous down leg or previous up leg and then closes above the previous low. Both condition warrant the stock is in a strong position. This triggers the buy signal. Confirmation of a bottom is produced when Ord-Volume increases 50 percent or more on the up leg after the bottom compared to the down leg going into the bottom.

I have found that the higher the percentage of shrinkage of average daily volume versus the previous up leg or down leg, the stronger the signal that is generated.

Sell Signals

Let's begin our discussion with sell signals, in particular looking at the strength of a signal generated based on the decline, or shrinkage, of average daily volume compared with previous up or down legs. Figure 3.7 illustrates this concept with the hypothetical stock "ABC." On the initial up leg, Ord-Volume is 100 million as the stock rises to a swing high of $50. After a brief pullback, "ABC" rallies again and puts in a modestly higher new high of $50.25 on average daily volume of 25 million. The stock then closes below $50, triggering a sell signal. Had we been following this stock, we would have been looking for the sell signal. Why? Because average daily volume on the second up leg was 75 percent less than the average daily volume on the first up leg.

Now, let's take a look at another example: The hypothetical stock "XYZ" shown in Figure 3.8. In this example, the stock has average daily volume of 100 million as it rallies to a swing high of $50. After a brief

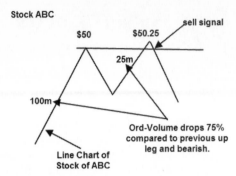

FIGURE 3.7 Average Daily Volume Comparisons for Sequential Up Legs for Stock "ABC"

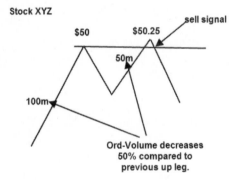

FIGURE 3.8 Average Daily Volume Comparisons for Sequential Up Legs for Hypothetical Stock "XYZ"

decline, XYZ rallies again to $50.25—just as stock ABC did. The average daily volume on the up leg to the second high, however, was 50 million for stock XYZ—or 50 percent less than the average daily volume for the previous up leg. The stock closes below $50, and a sell signal is triggered.

Comparing the changes in average daily volume for the two stocks, you can see that ABC is in a weaker position than XYZ. The reason is average daily volume on the second up leg for stock ABC was 75 percent less (25 million) on a break to a new high, while XYZ saw a 50 percent decline (50 million). This illustrates a key point: The magnitude of decline in average daily volume between up legs or down legs determines the strength of the buy or sell signal. And, as the percentage of decline in average daily volume falls below 50 percent, so does the reliability of the signal.

Let's review: A sell signal is triggered when a stock closes below a previous high and Ord-Volume on the second up leg shrinks by 50 percent or more compared with the previous up leg or down leg. Both conditions warrant a strong signal.

I want to emphasize that the average daily volume comparisons are between the final leg going into the top and the previous up leg *or* down leg immediately preceding the final leg.

Figure 3.9 shows a volume comparison of an up leg and a down leg in the movements of hypothetical stock "ZZZ." After a high is put in at $50 the stock declines on average daily volume of 100 million. The stock then rallies to a new high of $50.25 on average daily volume of 50 million. The Ord-Volume comparison of the up leg to a new high versus the previous down leg shows a 50 percent decline in volume. Once again, this meets the criteria for a sell signal, with average daily volume declining by at least 50 percent.

Now that the high has been determined using the Ord-Volume method, let's look at how that signal is confirmed. To confirm a high, we need to see energy (the force of the volume) switch from up to down. In other words, Ord-Volume needs to increase on the next down leg after the top is put in, compared with the previous up leg going into the top. That shows that energy is now pushing more strongly to the downside.

The percentage increase in average daily volume on the next down leg after the top also tells a lot about the strength of the signal. I like to see a 50 percent increase in Ord-Volume on the down leg after the top, compared with the up leg going into the top. A 50 percent increase is a minimum for a successful topping signal. Anything less than 50 percent sets up a higher probability that the stock will go back and retest the top.

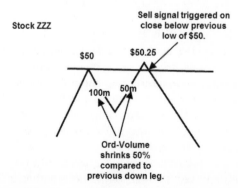

FIGURE 3.9 Ord-Volume Comparisons for the Final Up Leg to a New High versus the Previous Down Leg for Hypothetical Stock "ZZZ"

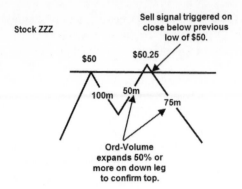

FIGURE 3.10   Sell Signal Is Triggered in Hypothetical Stock ZZZ Following a Close below the High, and a 50 Percent Increase in Average Daily Volume on the Next Down Leg Confirms the Top

Figure 3.10 shows that average daily volume on the down leg after the top at $50.25 is 75 million—an increase of 50 percent in volume from the previous up leg of 50 million.

Ideally, we would like to see Ord-Volume on the down leg increase by more than 100 percent after a top, compared to the previous up leg in order to show without a doubt that energy has switched from the upside to the downside. I will show a couple of examples where Ord-Volume increases substantially on the down leg after a top, and there was no looking back.

Figure 3.11 shows the strong up leg in November 2003 in BGO, with average daily volume of 8.24 million, as the stock put in a top at $4.23. The market then fell back on average daily volume of 5.67 million, which was followed by another rally that took the market to a new high at $4.30 on average daily volume of 2.85 million.

As we can see, on the last rally to $4.30, the energy to the upside was exhausted. In order to push this stock higher, more volume needed to be present, at least equal in magnitude to the previous up leg. By comparing the previous moves, we can see that the energy on the final up leg to the new high (2.85 million shares) was 65 percent less than the previous up leg (8.24 million shares). This meets the Ord-Volume criteria for a bearish signal. Also notice that the down leg from the high at $4.23 had an average daily volume of 5.67 million shares. Compared with this move, the next up leg had average daily volume of 2.85 million, which is 50 percent less— another bearish setup. A close below the previous high of $4.23 triggered a sell signal.

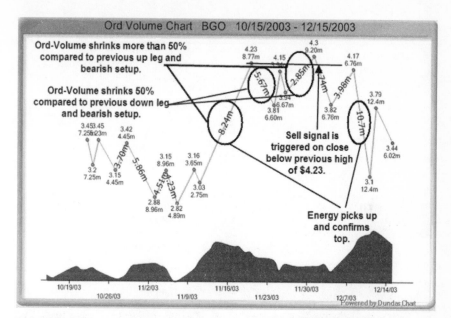

FIGURE 3.11   Ord-Volume Comparisons Show Average Daily Volume for Rally in Bema Gold (BGO) in November 2003, Followed by Subsequent Pullbacks and Rallies

To recap, a sell signal was triggered by the Ord-Volume method with a decline of 50 percent or more in average daily volume in the up leg to a new high compared with a previous up leg or down leg. The thrust to a new high at the $4.30 level in BGO on sharply reduced average daily volume showed that the upward energy had been depleted. The Ord-Volume analysis identified that condition. As Figure 3.11 also shows, BGO later fell to $3.10 on average daily volume of 10.7 million shares, confirming the top.

Topping Patterns   Yahoo Inc. (YHOO) had an interesting topping pattern in 2000. Figure 3.12 shows this movement in Ord-Volume format. During the rally from December 1999 into January 2000, as YHOO put in its high a $500.13, Ord-Volume decreased significantly to 25.4 million shares, compared to the previous up legs in November 1999. In fact, Ord-Volume going into the $500.13 high was about half the volume of the up legs in November 1999.

Notice that after the $500.13 high, on the next down leg Ord-Volume increased by 325 percent compared to previous up leg. This shows that energy had switched decisively from upward to downward, confirming

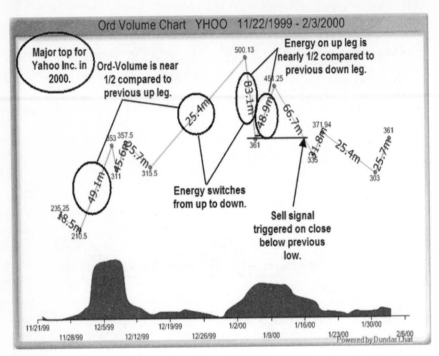

FIGURE 3.12   Ord-Volume Analysis of Major Top Put in Yahoo (YHOO) in Early 2000

the top. Sometimes the market tries to retest a high, but if there is not enough energy to reach a previous high, then the move will fail. This can be seen on the next up move in mid-January 2000. The stock tries to rally, but on low average daily volume (48.9 million shares) that is near half the volume of the preceding down leg. The market failed to generate enough energy to retest the previous high.

Let's review how sell signals are triggered using the Ord-Volume methodology:

- A sell signal is triggered when a stock closes below a previous high and the Ord-Volume (average daily volume) declines by 50 percent or greater compared with a previous up leg or down leg.
- Confirmation of a top is produced when Ord-Volume increases by 50 percent or more on the down leg after the top, compared to the up leg going into the top.

Other indicators can also be used in conjunction with Ord-Volume. In Figure 3.13, trend line analysis is applied to the Ord-Volume format.

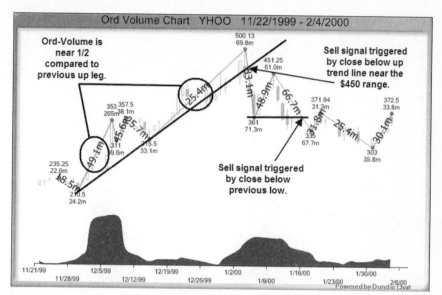

FIGURE 3.13 Trend-Line Analysis Applied to Ord-Volume Format Identifies Sell Signal for Yahoo (YHOO) Based on Close Below Trend Line

The chart for YHOO shows a trend line connecting the lows going back to the late November 1999 low. Since we knew that YHOO was in a weak position because of Ord-Volume analysis going into the $500.13 high, we could assume that the upside momentum would be broken by a close below this trend line, which would be around the $450 range. This sell signal at $450 was much closer to the high than a previous price target based on an old high at $357.50.

In Figure 3.14 (which displays YHOO prices after a split), a sell signal is generated here by a bearish crossover of the moving average convergence/divergence (MACD), an indicator that was invented by Gerald Appel. This type of sell signal using MACD also would have been triggered close to the top.

Examining the "Prevailing Force" One way in which to use Ord-Volume is to identify the direction of a stock by examining the prevailing force or energy, as illustrated by average daily volume. If you know that the energy is predominantly upward or downward, you can make better investment decisions. In the case of YHOO, the down leg after the $500.13 top had more than three times the Ord-Volume than the previous up leg. That said loudly and clearly that the energy in this stock had switched from the upside to the downside, giving confidence to sell. Once you have

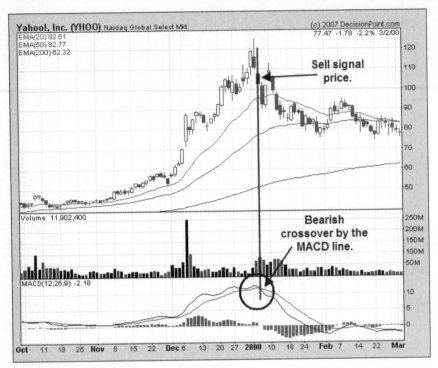

FIGURE 3.14   MACD Bearish Crossover Generates Sell Signal in YHOO Close to the Top
Source: Chart courtesy of DecisionPoint.com.

analyzed the energy in a particular stock or index based on Ord-Volume, you can use traditional indicators or your own system to target buy and sell signals.

Here's another example of a sell signal triggered by the Ord-Volume method. Figure 3.15 shows Novamerican Steel Inc. (TONS), which saw a steady upward move to a high of $90 a share and then turned down sharply. There were no bearish chart patterns (such as "head and shoulders") at the high that would have helped to identify a top.

Looking at TONS during the same time frame using Ord-Volume, however, it is much easier to see what was occurring as the stock approached the $90 level. Figure 3.16 shows that on the up leg going into the $90 top average daily volume had dropped to 113,000, compared to the previous up leg that had average daily volume of 296,000, which is nearly 60 percent less. This shows that the stock was in a weak position.

A close below the previous high of $74.85 triggers the sell signal. Notice, too, that on the down leg from the $90 high, Ord-Volume nearly

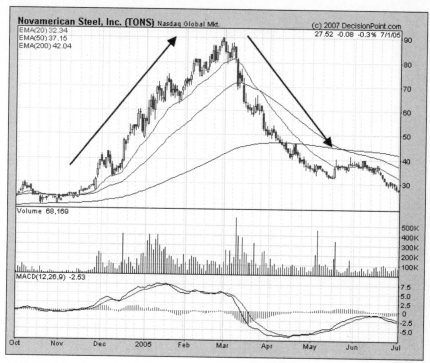

FIGURE 3.15 Price Chart Shows Sharp Rise and Then Fall in Novamerican Steel (TONS)
Source: Chart courtesy of DecisionPoint.com.

doubles, with average daily volume of 225,000 compared with 113,000 for the preceding up leg. Energy had clearly switched from the upside to the downside, confirming the top. This example shows what strong an influence volume has on price direction.

Based on the Ord-Volume analysis, a trader would have been alerted that a top had been put in—or was near. (A retest of the high, after all, would have been possible.) To make a trade closer to the top, we could use trend-line analysis. Figure 3.17 shows an up trend line connecting the low going back to November 2004. A sell signal is generated by a close below this up trend line and would have come not far from the top, around $85 a share. Once the trend line was broken, a trader would have assumed that the upside momentum was broken. Seeing volume increase on the down leg from the $90.27 high—as energy switched from the upside to the downside—a trader would have confidence that the trade would be profitable.

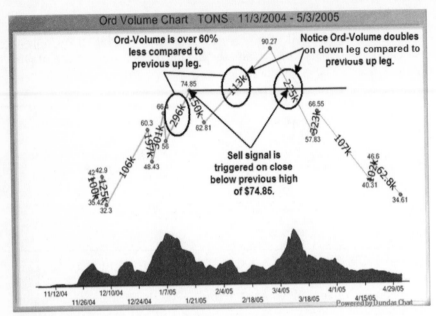

FIGURE 3.16   Ord-Volume Chart for Novamerican Steel (TONS) Shows Decline in Up Leg to the High at $90.27 Compared with Previous Up Leg

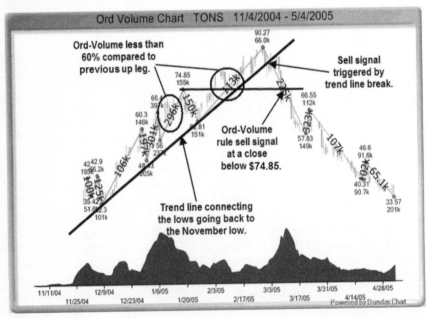

FIGURE 3.17   Trend Line on Chart for Novamerican Steel (TONS) Identifies Sell Signal

Buy Signals Generated by Ord-Volume

Now that we've looked at how sell signals are generated, it's time to switch to buy signals. Once again, the key factor is a comparison of Ord-Volume (average daily volume).

A buy signal is triggered when a stock hits a minor new low and Ord-Volume on the down leg shrinks by approximately 50 percent or greater against the previous down leg or previous up leg; the stock then closes above the previous low. Both conditions indicate the stock is in a strong position. Confirmation of a bottom is produced when Ord-Volume increases by 50 percent or more on the up leg after the bottom compared to the down leg going into the bottom.

Let's take a look at how this works using a hypothetical example: stock "EDF." Figure 3.18 shows EDF declines to $50 a share on Ord-Volume of 100 million shares.

In this example, EDF rallies and then declines again—with Ord-Volume on the second down leg of 25 million shares, putting in a new low at $49.50. You can see that the average daily volume is 75 percent less on the second down leg compared with the first. In this instance, a buy signal is triggered on a close above the previous low of $50 a share. Because the energy in this stock had switched from the downside to the upside, Ord-Volume increases on the subsequent up leg—in this instance a 300 percent increase to 75 million shares compared with the volume of the previous down leg of 25 million shares.

Figure 3.19 shows hypothetical stock "MNO" with average daily volume on a down leg of 100 million shares to a low of $50 a share, then a rally and a break to a new low of $49.50 a share. Volume on that second down leg declined by 50 percent compared with the previous down leg. The rally from the low at $49.50 had a 50 percent increase in Ord-Volume compared to previous down leg and confirmed the bottom.

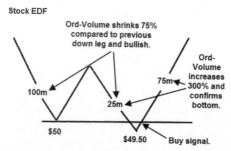

FIGURE 3.18 Ord-Volume Analysis for Hypothetical Stock "EDF" Shows Buy Signal Generated by Decline in Average Daily Volume on Sequential Down Legs

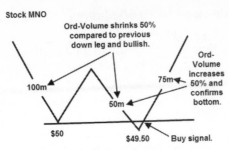

FIGURE 3.19 Ord-Volume Analysis of Hypothetical Stock MNO Shows 50 Percent Decline on Second Down Leg Compared with Previous Down Leg

Now compare the performance of the two stocks, EDF and MNO. For the first stock, EDF, average daily volume on two subsequent down legs declined by 75 percent. On MNO, the average daily volume declined by 50 percent. This shows that the energy to the downside was less on EDF than MNO; therefore, EDF had a stronger buy signal setup. EDF also had a 300 percent increase in Ord-Volume after the buy signal compared to MNO's 50 percent increase, which showed that EDF should outperform MNO on the rally phase.

To recap, the definition of a buy signal using the Ord-Volume methodology is: A buy signal is triggered when a stock closes above a previous low and Ord-Volume on the down leg declines by 50 percent or more compared with the previous up leg or previous down leg. Both conditions indicate the stock is in a strong position.

Figure 3.20 illustrates the buy signal concept graphically. Here, hypothetical stock "AAA" rallies from a low of $50 a share with Ord-volume on

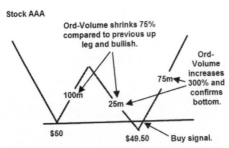

FIGURE 3.20 Buy Signal in Hypothetical Stock "AAA" Generated on a 75 Percent Decline in Ord-Volume on Sequential Down Legs

an up leg of 100 million shares, and then a decline to a new low at $49.50 on Ord-Volume of 25 million shares.

This example illustrates the rule for determining a buy signal using Ord-Volume. There is a decline in average daily volume on a down leg of 50 percent or more to confirm that a bottom is in place and that energy has switched to the upside. In fact, Ord-Volume on the up leg after the buy signal at 75 million shares is three times the volume on the previous down volume. Comparing the performance of AAA after the bottom is put in with stock MNO, you can see that AAA is a much stronger stock given the magnitude of the force to the upside.

Volume relationships between up legs and down legs are all about energy and how hard that force is pushing up or down. Understanding these Ord-Volume relationships, traders will more easily confirm or deny buy and sell setups. They also will see stronger and weaker buy and sell signals, enabling them to pick the stronger setups.

Figure 3.21 is an Ord-Volume chart of BGO, showing the average daily volume for the up legs and down legs as significant highs and lows are put in the stock.

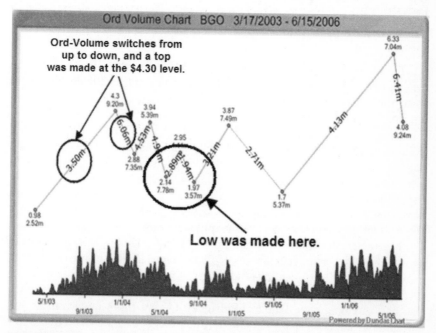

FIGURE 3.21   Ord-Volume Chart of Bema Gold (BGO) with Average Volume on Up Legs and Down Legs

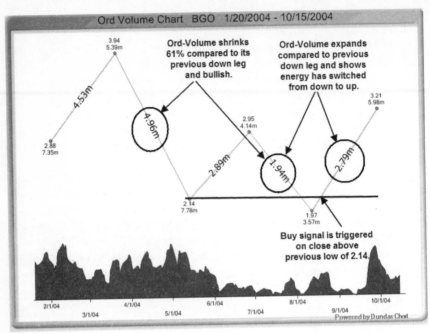

FIGURE 3.22   Ord-Volume on Bema Gold (BGO) Focuses on Time Frame when Significant Low Was Put in Place

Focus on the area in Figure 3.21 labeled "low was made here." This time frame is more detailed in Figure 3.22. Let's start with the down leg from the $2.95 price level in late June 2004. Ord-Volume on this down leg was 1.94 million shares.

Compare that down leg volume of 1.94 million shares with the Ord-Volume of the previous down leg of 4.96 million shares. This is a 61 percent decline in Ord-Volume and a bullish sign. A close above the previous low of $2.14 a share triggers a buy signal. On the rally up leg from the low, Ord-Volume expands to 2.79 million shares, compared with the previous down leg, showing that energy has switched from downward to upward. Once again, you can see how volume pushes price.

Figure 3.23 is a candlestick chart of 8 × 8 Inc. (EGHT). The price pattern shows a steady decline to a low of $1.32 and then a strong upward move.

Just looking at the candlestick chart alone, going into the $1.50 price level you would have no evidence that this would be the low (although you can obviously see that in hindsight). In real time, however, all you would have seen is a sharp decline in price. To get an indication that a low is being put in place, you would need to look at Ord-Volume, as depicted in Figure 3.24.

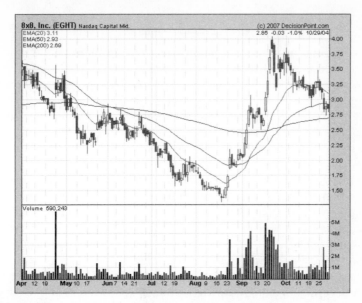

FIGURE 3.23 Candlestick Price Chart of 8 × 8 Inc. (EGHT)
Source: Chart courtesy of DecisionPoint.com.

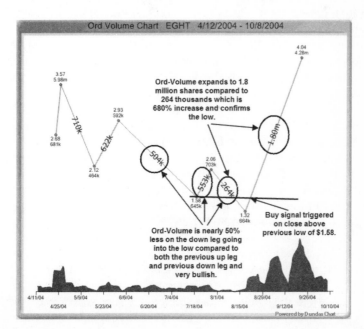

FIGURE 3.24 Ord-Volume Chart for 8 × 8 Inc. (EGHT) Showing Decline in Volume on Sequential Down Legs

THE BULLISH SETUP

The Ord-Volume analysis shows that volume is shrinking as the low is put in place. In the next chapter, we will explore how volume should behave as new lows or new highs are made. But for now, we will reply on price and volume alone.

As EGHT broke to a new low at $1.32, a trader would have see that Ord-Volume on the final down leg at 264,000 shares (Figure 3.24) was about half compared with the previous Ord-Volume down leg of 504,000 shares, and nearly 50 percent less than the Ord-Volume for the previous up leg of 553,000. This is a trigger for a bullish setup. The buy signal was triggered on a close above the previous low of $1.58. Notice that on the next up leg Ord-Volume explodes with a 680 percent increase in volume on the up leg to 1.80 million shares compared with the previous down leg volume of 264,000. This example shows how important it is for Ord-Volume to expand after a buy signal is triggered to confirm an uptrend. Further, in this example, an increase in Ord-Volume of this magnitude (nearly seven-fold compared with the previous down leg) implies that the rally will generate a big increase in price. The stock was up 255 percent in about one month.

A huge volume increase means there is huge energy, and that translates into a potential for a huge price move. Think back to the car analogy from the beginning of the chapter. When you push on the gas pedal a little, the car accelerates slowly. When you floor it, the car takes off rapidly.

Figure 3.25 shows EGHT in a different time frame at a different low. On the down leg going into the low at $0.65, Ord-Volume declined by 46 percent to 361,000 compared with the previous up leg volume of 642,000, as well as the previous down leg volume of 642,000. This triggers a bullish setup.

Ideally, the decline in Ord-Volume on a down leg going into a low—compared with a previous up leg or down leg—would be 50 percent or more. In the EGHT example, the 46 percent decline was still a bullish sign, and a close above the previous low at $0.85 triggered a buy signal. What Ord-Volume identified going into the $0.65 low was that the downward force had evaporated, and there was no more energy pushing the stock lower.

The stock's ability to close above its previous lows showed what little buying it took to move the stock higher. This is simply how the market works. When downward force evaporates because sellers of the stock have retreated to the sidelines, the stock will either go sideways or go up. What Ord-Volume identified in the case of EGHT was that the downward force had ended.

After the buy signal was triggered on a close above $0.85 a share, the stock drifted higher. As Figure 3.25 showed, volume began to expand

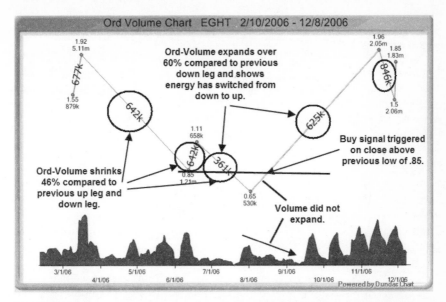

FIGURE 3.25 Ord-Volume Analysis Shows a Bullish Setup in 8 × 8 (EGHT)

toward mid-September and stayed strong into mid-November. Notice the expansion of volume on the rally phase after the buy signal on the current example, which is not as strong as the previous buy signal in Figure 3.24. The reason is in the previous example EGHT had a volume explosion of 680 percent after the buy signal, and EGHT jumped 256 percent in about a month.

In the current example, EGHT showed volume expanded 60 percent and the stock rallied 230 percent after the buy signal, but that took nearly three months. What this shows is the relationship of expanding volume of the same stock at two different time frames.

The higher energy—meaning a bigger the percentage increase in Ord-Volume on a rally leg after the buy signal—shown in Figure 3.24 produced faster results and a bigger percentage gain compared to the buy signal in Figure 3.25. It's all about the physics of stocks; the greater the energy force, the farther stocks go.

Figure 3.26 examines the continuation of the move in EGHT after the up phase ends. After a high was made at $1.96 a share, Ord-Volume on the down leg increased by 35 percent compared to the previous up leg, which suggested that energy may have switched from up to down. What this indicated was that either a top was made, or that a sideways consolidation is about to begin. There are three possible directions that a stock can move in: up, down, or sideways. With a 35 percent increase in Ord-Volume

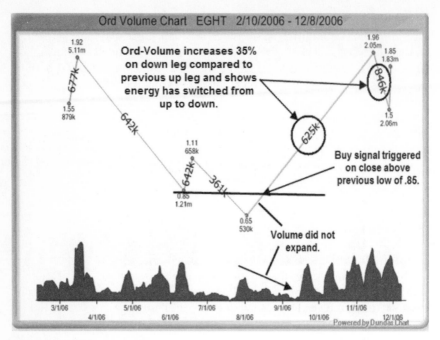

FIGURE 3.26   Ord-Volume Analysis of 8 × 8 (EGHT) after a High Was Put in at
$1.96

on the down leg, the up phase was likely over for EGHT. If someone was
holding the stock at this point, it would be time to look for an exit.

One clue may have been the smaller swings in EGHT near the highs.
However, if a trader had not looked at those smaller swings, he might still
be holding this stock. The bigger swing down from the high of $1.96 with
increased Ord-Volume suggested that a large-degree consolidation or a
down swing was beginning.

CONCLUSION

I have based a lot of my volume analysis on the work of trading master
Richard Wyckoff, who was famous in the 1930s for his abilities to forecast
stocks (as I explained in Chapter 1). Wyckoff was one of the first to find
the price–volume relationship. What I have done is expanded on Wyckoff's
ideas, simplified some, and added new ones. I made the Ord-Volume dis-
covery by studying Wyckoff's methods. We will cover some of his techniques in the next chapter.

Going back to the last example of EGHT, the 35 percent increase in Ord-Volume on the down leg off the $1.96 high suggested that it was time to exit the stock. Wyckoff would have called this expanded volume a "sign of weakness" (SOW). After a SOW, there is usually about a 50 percent retracement back toward the high, and this would be a good place to sell EGHT.

In the examples in this chapter, volume provided clues when a stock was nearing a low or a high. To successfully set up trades, a thorough understanding of volume should be in your trading arsenal. Thinking of volume as energy, one will understand how volume pushes price.

Trades that are set up by volume analysis, however, need to follow the signals of the general market. Don't expect to be profitable on bullish signals on stocks if the general market is in a downtrend, along with the sectors you are trading. And, don't expect your short signals on a stock to be profitable if the general market and the sectors you are trading are in an uptrend.

For the volume setup to work to your advantage, both the general market and your sector should be going in your direction. It's common sense—and that has a lot to do with stock trading.

CHAPTER 4

Price and Volume Relationships

As we learned in Chapter 3, using average daily volume—or Ord-Volume, as I call it—we can measure and compare the strength of one leg to another. This volume analysis also can be applied to swings to tell you if the market has the strength to pass through a previous swing or if it is likely to reverse. (To refresh, a *swing* is the point at which a stock, index, or other issue changes direction. A *leg* is the distance between two swings.) Previous swing areas are important to watch for strength or weakness. The way to tell whether the market is likely to pass through a previous swing high or low is by volume analysis.

Stocks develop trading ranges because a particular issue does not have enough strength to get through its previous swing high or its previous swing low. As stated in Chapter 3, what it takes to get through a previous high or low is energy. *Energy*, as we defined it, is the amount of volume that is pushing the price up or down. Put another way, the energy of the stock is reflected in how high or low the volume is. Now, a lot of traders will say that a stock had "good volume" on a particular day; say, one million shares. What does that really mean? By itself it does not mean anything, and, in fact, statements like these miss the point of what the stock volume is *really* saying.

Volume is always analyzed by comparing; it can be to previous legs or swings. The idea of volume analysis is to look for increases or decreases compared to previous swings or legs to identify whether there is an increase or decrease in strength. Stocks need an "energy source" in order to be propelled forward. That energy is volume. When the energy runs out, it will reverse. A trader should identify and understand which way the energy is pushing, and watch areas where the energy starts to reverse. That way, a trader will be better able to profit.

Don't make the process of stock trading more complicated by introducing factors that have little or no effect on stock price. Information overload is a common downfall in stock analysis. Keep it simple. Volume alone will tell you which way the force is pushing the stock. If a news announcement on a stock is released, then the volume (buying or selling) will make the right interpretation for the announcement—whether bullish or bearish—because people in the know will push the stock in its true direction. Therefore, the true interpretation of the news announcement will show up in the volume analysis. Personally, that is why I have little regard for fundamental analysis, because you don't know what points about the company are exaggerated and what points (if negative) are minimized. However, the true interpretation will show up in the volume analysis.

By following the direction of the highest volume, a trader is actually following the "smart money." Smart money is well capitalized and, therefore, has the means to produce the most volume. And, smart money produces the most money by being correct in the market. Therefore, if you can follow the direction of the highest volume, you can follow the smart money. To me, that is all the fundamental analysis you need to know. In my seminars, I talk about stocks by their symbols only; I don't even focus on the name of the company. The reason is that when I'm trading a stock, the name doesn't matter to me. I only need to know the symbol so I can pull it up on my quote system and analyze its price and volume.

It does matter to me, however, what sector the stock is in, because—as stated in Chapter 2—the sector also has to be bullish in order for me to be trading a particular stock. Other than that, the price and volume of the stock tells me what I need to know if I want to own it. I don't get bogged down with information such as where the company is located, the number of employees, and so on. This type of information, to me, does not have a bearing on stock direction. The only thing that generates profits in the market is to know stock direction. Volume analysis will help find stock direction.

VOLUME ANALYSIS AT SWINGS

The first rule of volume analysis at swings deals with a very important concept: percentage relationship. We do not focus on the amount of the volume, but rather the comparison—on a percentage basis—of the volume versus a previous swing high or low.

Here is the rule:

It is not the amount of the volume that is important at previous swing highs or lows, but rather the percentage relationship *compared with the previous high or low. These volume percentage relationships will determine if the market will pass through or reverse at these previous highs or lows.*

Let's go one step further: To get a buy signal, a test is needed of a previous swing low and the volume must shrink by 8 percent or more, and then close back above the previous low. This condition will trigger the buy signal. A test means *breaking* the previous swing low to prove the point.

To get a sell signal, a test is needed of a previous swing high and the volume must shrink by 8 percent or more, and then close back below the previous high. This condition will trigger the sell signal. A test means *breaking* the previous swing high to prove the point.

These volume percentage relationships work on all time frames: 60 minutes, daily, weekly, or monthly. I might add that the higher the percentage decrease in volume on the retest of a previous high or low, the more reliable and stronger the signal will be for a reversal. That makes sense because if the energy is significantly less than at the previous high, there will also be less force, which means a safer trade for a reversal.

Let's take a look at an example. Figure 4.1 shows a line chart of the hypothetical stock "ABC." I call this trade setup "low volume retest."

There is only one safe place to take trades and that is at or near a previous high or low. Think of the examples in Chapter 3 in which Ord-Volume buy and sell signal setups were taken on trades on a close above a previous low or below a previous high. In theory, if a market can't hold below a previous low, then it is bullish. Similarly, if a market can't hold above a previous high, then it is bearish. Charts of the market are not randomly formed but are structured by tests of previous highs and lows, with the

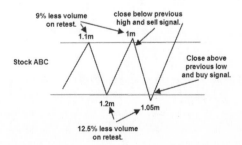

FIGURE 4.1   Low Volume Retest Trade Setup for Stock "ABC"

market going in the direction of the highest energy. If a market runs into a previous high that has more volume than the current rally, then that high will be rejected, and vice versa.

Notice that I am giving volume equal status with price. Both volume and price must meet certain requirements to trigger a buy or sell signal. Now you have double confirmation for a signal to be triggered, and that is with price and volume. To illustrate, Figure 4.2 shows a sell signal triggered by this method on a weekly chart of Research in Motion Ltd. (RIMM).

Similarly, Figure 4.3 illustrates a buy signal triggered for RIMM, also using a weekly chart. Figure 4.3 also shows a sell signal triggered a few months later, also by the retest method.

Once a sell signal is triggered, the next downside target is the previous low. Therefore, a trader also knows what price is likely to become the next possible reversal point in the market. If the next swing low is tested

FIGURE 4.2   Sell Signal Triggered for Research in Motion (RIMM) with Retest of Previous High and Decline in Volume
Source: Chart courtesy of DecisionPoint.com.

FIGURE 4.3 Buy Signal Triggered for Research in Motion (RIMM) with Retest of Previous Low and Decline in Volume, Followed by a Sell Signal Triggered by the Retest Method
Source: Chart courtesy of DecisionPoint.com.

on equal or higher volume, then the downtrend remains intact, and the trader has reason to hold a short position. For a buy signal, the upside target is the previous high. If that high is tested on equal or higher volume, then energy is continuing to push higher, and the trader has a reason to hold a long position.

If you think these conditions through, you will see that what you are actually doing is following the way that the energy is pushing the strongest. Also remember that, whatever stock you are trading, you should be aligned with the overall direction of the market—and you should be in one of the best sectors (see Chapter 2). This alignment is like "putting the wind at your back," and it is very important to remember this factor. Being aligned with the market and the best sectors—to switch metaphors for a moment—will put "the wind in your sails," and will likely carry your positions farther and faster than you would otherwise experience.

This concept of keeping the "wind at your back" will be repeated in upcoming chapters. It's worth repeating because this is one of the main mistakes that traders make. Traders must always know what the broader market—as represented by the S&P 500, Nasdaq, and NYSE—is doing. Being aligned to the market and being in the best sectors will increase your chances of trading successfully "with the wind at your back."

High-Volume Retest

There are several variations of volume analysis at swings. The first one we'll cover here is High-Volume Retest, as shown in Figure 4.4. This chart shows hypothetical stock "EDF" as a previous high is retested.

As this example shows, the volume on the retest is 97 million—just 3 percent below the volume at the previous swing high of 100 million. The rule here is that if on the retest of a previous swing high volume declines by only 3 percent or less, it implies that upside energy is good and the market should continue its rally. In other words, volume that is very near or equal to the previous high (97 percent or more) indicates the presence of upside energy that is strong enough to push the market higher. The stock may pull back from a previous high a little before heading higher, but the condition remains bullish.

Reversals are expected on test of highs when volume is 92 percent or less than the volume at the previous high. Therefore, if volume is nearly equal (declining by only 3 percent or less) than the volume at the previous high, the market has energy to exceed the previous high. However, if volume shrinks down to 92 percent or less (a decline of 8 percent or more in volume) on the current test of the previous highs, then energy is not adequate to get through the highs and the market should reverse.

Figure 4.5 is a weekly chart of Eldorado Gold Corporation (EGO). During the first two weeks of November 2006, EGO tested previous highs

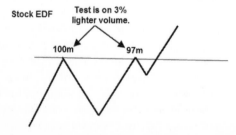

FIGURE 4.4   High-Volume Retest for Stock "EDF" Shows Good "Energy" to the Upside, with the Rally Likely to Continue

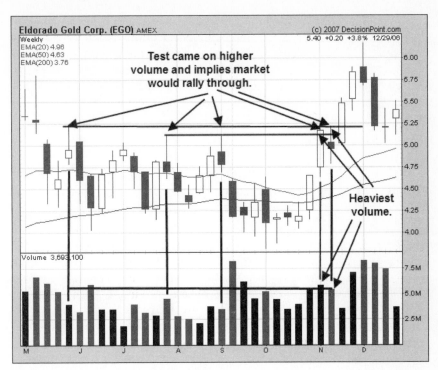

FIGURE 4.5   Weekly Chart of Eldorado Gold (EGO) Shows Higher Volume on Retests of Previous Highs, Indicating Stock Will Likely Rally, Which It Did after November Retest
Source: Chart courtesy of DecisionPoint.com.

going back to May of that year. All the previous highs were tested on higher volume, which implied EGO had energy to pass through the old high and rally higher. As the chart shows, that is exactly what the stock did.

Now let's look at what happens when the High-Volume Retest occurs at a previous low. The same theory is at work here, but in the opposite direction. Figure 4.6 shows hypothetical stock GHI testing a previous low on near-equal volume of 97 million shares, compared with 100 million on the previous retest. In other words, the volume is 97 percent, or has declined by only 3 percent. This condition suggests that the stock has enough energy to pass through the previous low and continue lower.

Now let's take a look at an actual example. Figure 4.7 is a daily chart of EGO, spotlighting the time frame of January through April 2005. Notice how the volume picks up at the previous lows, indicating the stock should continue to decline, which it does.

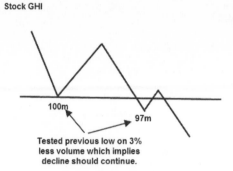

FIGURE 4.6 Chart of Hypothetical Stock GHI Shows Near-Equal Volume at Retest of Previous Low, Indicating Downtrend Should Continue

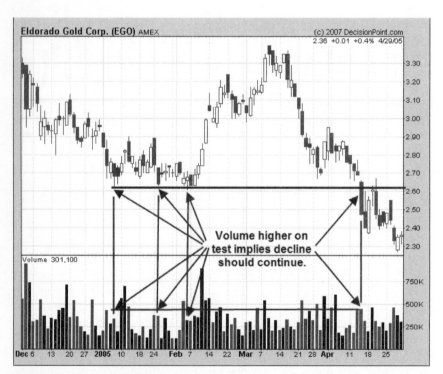

FIGURE 4.7 Daily Chart of Eldorado Gold (EGO) Shows Higher Volume on Retests of Previous Lows, Indicating the Downtrend Will Continue
Source: Chart courtesy of DecisionPoint.com.

First High Retest

Now it's time to look at a pattern that is more complicated in how it works. Figure 4.8 shows this pattern, known as First High Retest. The rule here is always to compare the volume relationships to the first high (or low), even on the third and fourth retests. The volume percent relationships on tests remain the same. They are:

- A volume decline of 3 percent or less on a test indicates that the move will continue.
- A volume decline of 8 percent or greater on a test indicates a reversal.

In Figure 4.8, at the first high (marked "A") volume comes in at 100 million. This is the first high against which all retests are compared. At retest, "B" volume is 96 million shares, which is a 4 percent decline. This means the stock is in "No Man's Land." It does not have enough energy to rally through the previous high because volume needs to be within a 3 percent decline or less. Nor has volume dropped by 8 percent or greater than the previous high, which would signal a reversal. Therefore, the market may just drift near its current high.

Another rally comes in at point "C" to retest the highs of "A" and "B." Volume at "C" of 95 million is compared to the volume at the first high at point "A." With volume at "C" that is 5 percent less than at "A," the stock is still in "No Man's Land," and no conclusions can be drawn.

At "D," the volume is 92 million shares, which, compared with the volume at the high at "A," is 8 percent less. Therefore, the retest at "D" on 8 percent lighter volume is a bearish sign, and a sell signal is triggered on a close below the high of "A." As this example showed, all previous highs after the "A" top were tested and compared to the volume at the first high at "A."

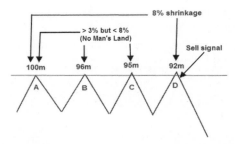

FIGURE 4.8   Chart Showing Volume Comparisons with First High to Illustrate the "First High Retest" Rules

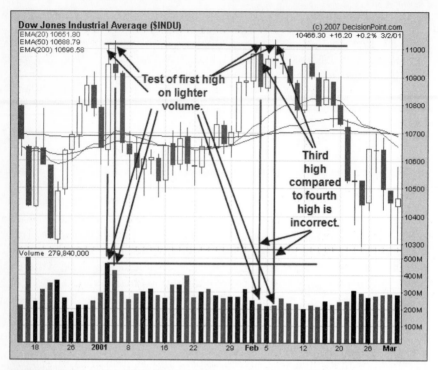

FIGURE 4.9   First High Retest in Dow Jones Industrial Average ($INDU) Shows
that the Correct Comparison of Volume Is to That of the First High
Source: Chart courtesy of DecisionPoint.com.

Figure 4.9 shows an example of a First High Retest using the Dow
Jones Industrial Average ($INDU). Once again, it is important to remem-
ber that the volume at the second, third, and fourth highs are tested
against the volume at the first high. Otherwise, a trader might compare the volume of the fourth high to that of the third high and would
not come up with the correct conclusion. For example, in Figure 4.9, if
a trader compared the fourth high's volume to the third high's volume,
the comparison would be about equal and would not have identified the
bearish setup that followed.

First Low Retest

The same setup also applies to bottoms. The volume of the second, third,
and fourth lows are always compared to the volume on the first low.
Figure 4.10 shows this setup, which is called the First Low Retest. The
rules are the same as for the First High Retest, but on the downside.

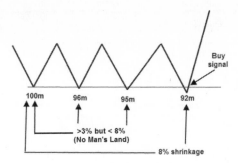

FIGURE 4.10   First Low Retest Shows the Volume Comparisons to the First Low

As Figure 4.10 shows, volume declines that are greater than 3 percent but less than 8 percent result in a "No Man's Land" condition. Once volume compared with the first low declines by 8 percent or greater, a buy signal is triggered.

Before going further, we need to consider a nuance in interpreting volume. When there is a sudden expansion in volume, it is a longer-term bearish sign but a short-term bullish sign. A sudden expansion in volume usually stops the trend, at least momentarily. This expansion in volume uses up all the energy for the short term and stops the trend. Sometime after a big expansion in volume, the trend may follow through for another day. However, that day shows a lot less volume. This is a common occurrence in the market. The price low is achieved one day after the big expansion in volume. In cases such as these, use the highest volume (energy) day for volume comparisons and use the highest (or lowest if trend is down) price of the day or the next day for swing comparisons.

To illustrate this point, look at Figure 4.11, which shows a chart of the S&P 500 ($SPX) that focuses on May 2005. Here, we are comparing the maximum energy (the highest volume day) to an extreme price range. Sometimes they do not fall on the same day but are still very close to each other.

Let move on to Figure 4.12 to see how a First Low Retest sets up. Notice that we are taking the price low day of May 18, 2005, and volume day from May 15, 2005. Also notice that the $SPX traded below the price low of May 18, 2005, twice and then closed above the May 18, 2005, low, and both of those days had less volume than May 15, 2005. These conditions showed the $SPX did not have enough energy to get through the May 18, 2005, price low and therefore triggered a buy signal.

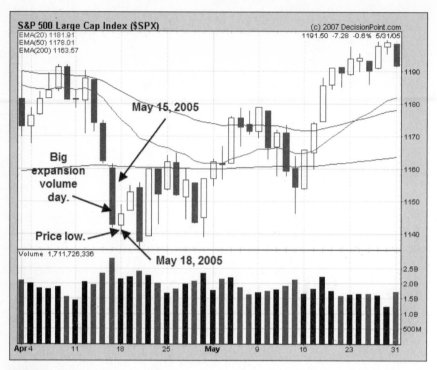

FIGURE 4.11   Chart of S&P 500 Shows Big Expansion Volume Day on May 15, Followed by a New Price Low in the Next Trading Session
Source: Chart courtesy of DecisionPoint.com.

Strength of a Signal on a Retest

The next point I want to cover is the power of a retest to determine the strength of a signal. In Figure 4.13, the issue trades above the previous high on 5 percent less volume and closes below the previous high. There is no assurance that this issue will turn down because the retest still had relatively good energy compared to its previous high, because volume declined by only 5 percent.

In Figure 4.14, however, this issue trades above its previous high on 20 percent less volume, and then turned down and closed below the previous high. The result is a strong sell signal. Since the issue had far less energy on the retest compared to its previous high, it is a much better candidate for a sell signal. A trader can identify the strength of a sell signal by the degree of volume shrinkage on the retest of its previous high.

On previous examples of test of highs (or lows), we used a minimum of 8 percent shrinkage against previous swing highs (or lows) to qualify a

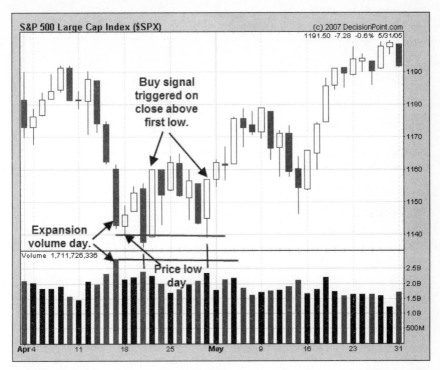

FIGURE 4.12   Chart of S&P 500 Shows Volume Comparison for May 15 and Price Low of May 18 as Basis for Buy Signal Setup
Source: Chart courtesy of DecisionPoint.com.

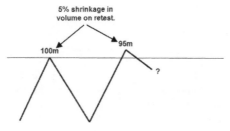

FIGURE 4.13   Comparison of Volume on a Retest Shows Good Energy Remains when Volume Declines by Only 5 Percent

successful outcome. The signal strength increases as the volume percentage decreases on the test of the previous swing high (or low). Therefore, if a trader has a choice between two issues, the stronger trade would be the one that has volume of 80 percent (meaning a 20 percent decline) on the retest compared to the first swing high (or low), rather than the issue that has volume of 95 percent (a 5 percent decline) on the retest

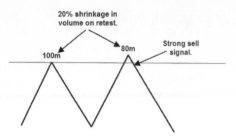

FIGURE 4.14 Comparisons of Volume on a Retest Shows the More Volume Declines, the Stronger the Signal Generated

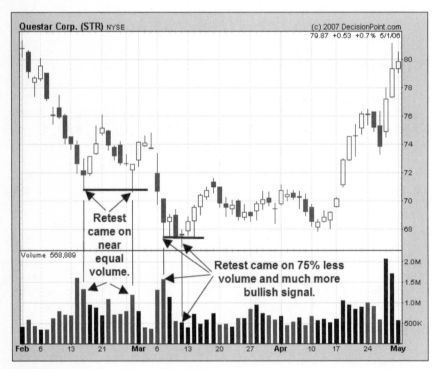

FIGURE 4.15 Volume Comparisons of Retest Low in Questar Corporation (STR), First at Near-Equal Volume and Later with a Greater Volume Reduction to Trigger a Buy Signal
Source: Chart courtesy of DecisionPoint.com.

compared to the first swing. Once again, we are using volume relation-ships to determine signal strength.

Let's take a look at Questar Corporation (STR) to show how these volume forces work in real life. As shown in Figure 4.15, in mid-February

2006, STR made a low near the $71 range. A retest of that level came at the end of February on a minor degree reduction in volume. The stock did rally for a couple of days then fell through the low at $71.

In early March STR made a low below $68 on expanded volume. A retest came three days later on about 75 percent less volume and produced a much stronger buy signal. As you can see in Figure 4.15, the March low was not touched again and STR continued a strong rally into April and May. Because of the much stronger volume relationships, the March low was the stronger buy signal and produced a much stronger rally compared to the February setup.

Equal Volume Retest

There are more rules on swings; the next one we're going to cover is "Equal Volume Retest." Figure 4.16 illustrates this rule and the trade setup involved. The retest at point "B" at 99 million is nearly equal to the volume at the previous high at "A" of 100 million. Since the rally energy did not really dissipate at "B" compared to the top at "A," the trend remains bullish. A pullback can form here, but it would likely be shallow. Then, after a minor pullback the market should stage another rally to point "C" because the rally energy is still in force.

At level "C," the volume should be near equal or higher than the volume at "A" and "B" in order to keep the uptrend intact, or the volume will have to decline by 8 percent or more in order for the market to turn down. (The same rules apply for lows.)

Let's take a look at the Equal Volume Retest in action in Figure 4.17. As you recall from Figure 4.15, a strong buy signal was triggered on STR. Figure 4.17 shows the continuation of that action following the buy signal. By late March 2006, the stock made a high near $71, with a retest of that

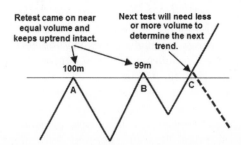

FIGURE 4.16   Equal Volume Retest at Point "B" Compared with Point "A" Sets Up Another Move to Point "C"

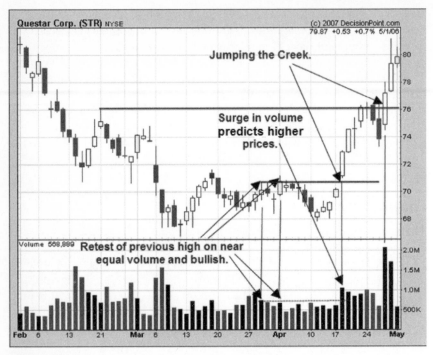

FIGURE 4.17   A Retest of the Late-March High in Questar (STR) in Early April on Nearly Equal Volume Keeps the Stock in a Bullish Trend
Source: Chart courtesy of DecisionPoint.com.

high on the first trading day in April with near-equal volume compared with the late March high, which kept STR in a bullish mode.

A retest of the previous highs occurred in mid-April, and the volume expanded compared to the previous high's volume, which predicted that the uptrend should resume—and it did. Richard Wyckoff, whose studies of price and volume were the basis of my Ord-Volume work, called this type of move—when the market jumps above the previous high on expanded volume—"Jumping the Creek." As Figure 4.17 shows, the mid-April rally in STR through the highs on expanding volume was "Jumping the Creek," and a bullish confirmation of the uptrend. Notice in late-April STR "jumped the creek" at the $76 level.

In this example, you can see how volume is the energy force behind price. These same rules apply for bottoms as well. Figure 4.18 shows "Equal Volume Retest" pattern on the rest of previous lows—with near-equal volume at the point "B" low compared with point "A," setting up for the retest at "C." If the volume at "C" is higher, the downtrend will continue. If the volume declines at point "C" by 8 percent or greater, the market will likely reverse to the upside.

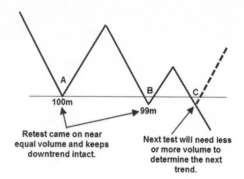

FIGURE 4.18 Equal Volume Retest of the Low at Point "B" Compared with the Volume at Point "A" Sets Up for the Retest at Point "C"

To illustrate, let's go back to the chart of STR, but this time for an earlier time frame—February 2006. In late February, STR tested a previous low made mid-month around $71 on near-equal volume, which kept the trend bearish. In early March, STR retested the $71 level on somewhat expanded volume, which implied that the market had enough energy to push through the lows, which it did (Figure 4.19). Richard Wyckoff called this pattern "Falling through Ice." However, if on the third test in early March at the $71 level, volume had declined by 8 percent or more versus the first low in mid-February, then the market would reverse. Remember, it's all about volume relationships and watching how volume reacts at previous price highs and lows.

False Breakout Tops

Another swing relationship is when the market breaks to new highs above the previous high on lighter volume that has declined by 8 percent or greater and then closes above the previous highs. This condition suggests a false breakout to the upside because the energy (volume) was not strong enough to suggest the rally will continue. Remember to keep a rally going; energy (volume) should be at least equal or higher than at the previous high. When energy shrinks and the market still moves higher above the previous highs then a top is nearing. This setup is just like a lighter volume retest of a previous high, but in this case the market closes above the previous high. I have named this setup "False Breakout Top."

In Figure 4.20, the market breaks out on 10 percent lighter volume (90 million versus 100 million at the previous high), implying a false break to the upside. A close below the previous high triggers the sell signal.

The chart of JP Morgan Chase & Company (JPM) in Figure 4.21 is a good example to illustrate the False Breakout Top principle. JPM created its first important high in late January 2007 at the $51.16 level. JPM

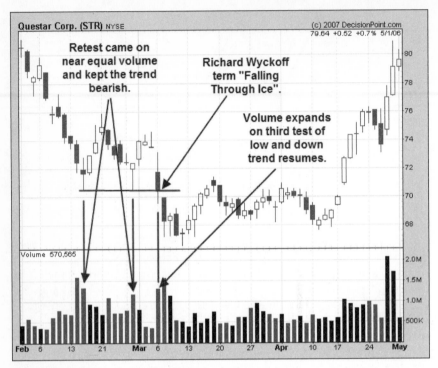

FIGURE 4.19 A Retest of the Low in Questar (STR) in February and March Shows the Equal Volume Retest Rule in Action
Source: Chart courtesy of DecisionPoint.com.

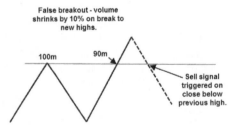

FIGURE 4.20 False Breakout Top Pattern Shows a Move above the Previous High on Lighter Volume

bumped along for more than a week then jumped above the previous important high of $51.16 on February 14 on much lighter volume and closed above the previous important high. This condition suggested that a false breakout had occurred, and the move was not a bullish condition.

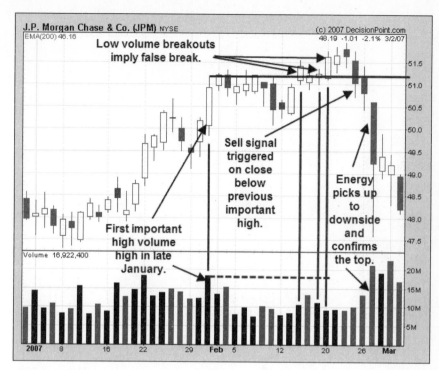

FIGURE 4.21   False Breakout Top Principle Illustrated in JP Morgan Chase (JPM)
Source: Chart courtesy of DecisionPoint.com.

Over the next several days JPM tried to move higher, but volume was comparatively low, which showed the upside energy was very weak. On February 23, the stock closed below the $51.16 high and triggered a sell signal. Notice how volume picked up to the downside after the sell signal day, which showed that energy was pushing to the downside and confirmed the sell signal.

False Breakout Bottom

The flipside is the False Breakout Bottom as illustrated in Figure 4.22. This pattern shows how volume shrank by 8 percent or more (92 million versus 100 million compared to the previous low) on a break to new lows. This indicated that a potential bullish signal may be setting up. A close above the previous low will trigger the buy signal.

Figure 4.23 is a weekly chart of JPM for a different time frame, focusing this time on mid- to late 2002. In mid-July, JPM put in a low at $18.22. JPM then rallied over several weeks before selling off and putting in a new

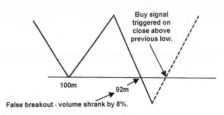

FIGURE 4.22　　　False Breakout Bottom Shows Retest of Low on Lower Volume

FIGURE 4.23　　　False Breakout Bottom Principle Illustrated in JPM
Source: Chart courtesy of DecisionPoint.com.

weekly low in September at $16.54—well below the mid-July low. Notice how the weekly volume shrank by more than 30 percent on the break to new lows. For a market to continue lower, volume should be near equal or higher than the previous low. In this case, volume was much lighter and suggested there was not enough energy to keep the downtrend intact.

Figure 4.23 also shows a buy signal was triggered a couple weeks later on a close above $18.22. Also notice we used a weekly time frame and the rules had the same results. The rules work on any time frame.

TRADING GAPS WITH VOLUME COMPARISONS

Gaps are a very important for trading. Gaps form on stocks and indexes where there is a price void. In other words, no transactions took place at that price level, and prices jumped over that level—or under that level, depending which way the market was moving. Gaps form all the time in stocks and indexes, and if you know how to handle them, you can make profitable decisions to take advantage of these events.

It is said that the market always goes back to "fill in" the gap. In my experience that is not always true. What I did discover in my price and volume studies is that the larger the gap and the higher the volume on the gap day, the more likely the gap will be tested. My studies of gaps also show that the smaller gaps with light volume are frequently left unfilled. Therefore, if the gap is wide and has high volume, then there is a very good likelihood that the gap will be tested again. Knowing this, a trader can take advantage of the potential setup.

As previously stated, gaps form on stocks and indexes where there is a price void. Almost always wide price gaps are accompanied by heavy volume as transactions to buy overwhelm transactions to sell, thereby creating a gap up (or transactions to sell overpower transactions to buy and a gap down is formed). If the gap is big and the volume is heavy, this is a setup for a trading opportunity. For now, we will work with a market that is rising, creating a gap up, although the same rules apply for a market that gaps down.

Usually when a market gaps on high volume, it represents a bullish condition on the larger time frames, but a bearish condition on the shorter-term time frames. When a gap forms on big volume, energy for that short-term event is used up. Normally, that market is near the end of that price rise or move, and may then begin a consolidation pattern.

Testing Upside Gaps

Gaps act like previous highs and lows: When a stock or index gaps up, then the gap itself turns into a support level for any pullback. Previous examples have shown trades that were triggered by a test of a previous high or low. Tests of gaps also trigger trades. Tests of gaps on lighter volume imply that the issue does not have enough energy to get through the gap; instead, the gap becomes support and a bullish signal is triggered.

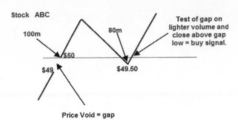

FIGURE 4.24   Gap Test Rules Show a Buy Signal Triggered by Lighter Volume on a Gap Test and Close above the Gap Low

In Figure 4.24 we have a line chart of stock ABC. A gap formed from $49 to $50 on trading volume of 100 million shares. ABC then pulls back to $49.50 on volume of 80 million shares, or 20 percent less volume than when the gap was formed. A close above the gap at $50 triggers the buy signal.

Here is the rule for buy signal on gaps ("Gap Test"):

Tests of gaps on a 10 percent or greater decrease in volume and a close above the gap low triggers a buy signal. The lighter the volume on the test of the gap the stronger the buy signal.

I have also found that the gap does not need to close completely for this trade set up to be successful. In the example of stock ABC, notice that the pullback to fill the gap came in at $49.50 and not all the way back to $49 to close the gap. In my studies, I have concluded that an issue only needs to break an area of the gap to have a bullish setup. Therefore, on the current example, even a pullback in stock ABC to $49.99 would have been sufficient to trigger a buy signal.

A gap may sometimes be tested more than once. As long as volume on the test of the gap declines by 10 percent or more, then the gap will hold, and the market should move higher. It is important to remember that a stronger signal is generated when volume is very light on the test of the gap. This condition shows that energy is very weak as the market tries to push through the gap level, and this, in turn, is very bullish for the issue.

If a trader has a choice between two issues that are each testing gaps levels, the trader should take the issue where volume shrinkage is the highest against the gap level as that will be the stronger setup. Shrinkage in volume of 10 percent on a test of a gap level is the minimum requirement in order to realize a positive result. Less than 10 percent shrinkage in volume on the gap test will lower the chances of a successful trade.

Figure 4.25 is a candlestick chart of Google, Inc. (GOOG). In late December 2006, GOOG tested the gap level from late October of $430 to $454 on nearly 50 percent lighter volume and then closed above the gap level. This condition triggered the buy signal. Notice that there were

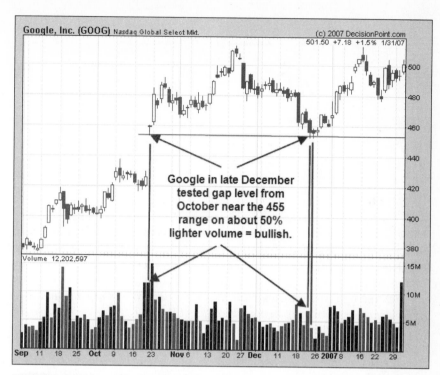

FIGURE 4.25   Gap Test in Google (GOOG) in December 2006 on Lighter Volume Triggered a Buy Signal
Source: Chart courtesy of DecisionPoint.com.

two tests of the gap level in late December, and both times buy signals were triggered. The second test in late December of the October gap was the stronger buy signal because the volume was much lighter than the first test (which was the day before). The second test showed there was less force to the downside and a more bullish condition existed. This buy signal at the $454 range had an upside target to the previous high of $513 range, and that target was achieved.

Downside Gaps

Now we will cover the flip side: gaps that form to the downside. Here is the rule for the sell signal on gaps ("Gap Test"):

> *Tests of gaps with a decrease in volume of 10 percent or greater and a close below the gap high triggers the sell signal. The lighter the volume on the test of the gap the stronger the sell signal.*

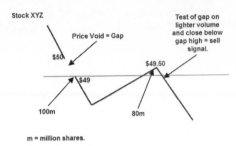

FIGURE 4.26   Gap Test on the Downside with Lighter Volume and a Close below the Gap High Triggers a Sell Signal

Figure 4.26 shows the gap test bearish setup, with the same principles as the bullish scenario. A high-volume gap forms on stock XYZ from $50 to $49 on trading volume of 100 million shares. A test of the gap level comes at $49.50 on 80 million shares. The gap test on 20 percent lighter volume compared to gap day volume of 100 million shares shows that energy is not high enough to get through the gap level; this is a bearish sign. Stock XYZ closes below the gap high and triggers the sell signal.

Figure 4.27 shows AMR Corporation (AMR), which, in late January 2007, gapped down on heavy volume of more than 30 million shares. AMR rallied back several times and tested the gap level near $38.50, but every time the market fell back. A test of the gap and a close below the high of the gap on lighter volume triggered a sell signal. In this example, four sell signals were triggered.

Notice how the gap level near the $38.50 to $40 range provided resistance on the rally attempts. The volume on the rallies into the gap level was about 80 percent lighter than the volume on the gap day; this showed in no uncertain terms that the market did not have enough energy to get through the gap level. In late February, AMR started to fall significantly.

Selling Climax Day

One of the strongest and most reliable signals generated is the "Selling Climax Day" signal. This trade setup is found where the market has been going down for at least several weeks, if not for several months. The down move then ends abruptly. The reason this signal works so well is that volume expands to such a degree that for the near term the down force is all used up and the market just stops.

The rule for a Selling Climax Day is volume expands by at least 20 percent or more compared with the days before and after. This surge of volume uses up all the downward energy for the short term and the market is halted. The Selling Climax Day is not the buy signal day; rather,

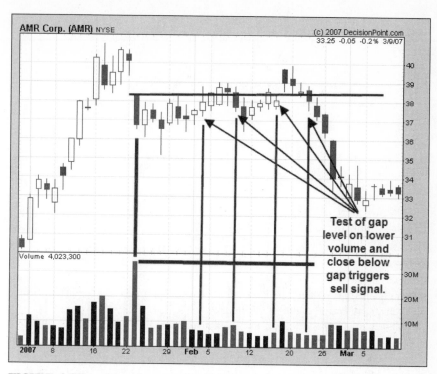

FIGURE 4.27 Test of a gap in AMR Corporation (AMR) on Lighter Volume and a Close below the Gap High Triggered a Sell Signal
Source: Chart courtesy of DecisionPoint.com.

the buy signal comes on the test of the low of the Selling Climax Day. The test of the Selling Climax Day low must be on at least 8 percent shrinkage in volume, followed by a close above the low of the Selling Climax Day; these conditions trigger the buy signal.

The Selling Climax Day signal is similar to the Low Volume Retest signal discussed in Figure 4.1. However, the Selling Climax Day signal has a higher degree of volume expansion the first day of the low, and therefore has more energy in the signal itself, which gives it more importance.

The Selling Climax Day signal produces significant rallies that usually last for several months. A trader should master this trade setup because all major lows in the past several years for the NYSE, S&P 500, and the Nasdaq Composite have been picked out with the Selling Climax Day signal. This is the setup that "puts the wind at your back" as you trade.

Figure 4.28 is the Selling Climax Day buy signal for the S&P 500 at the June and July 2006 low. Volume jumped to 3.2 billion shares on June 8,

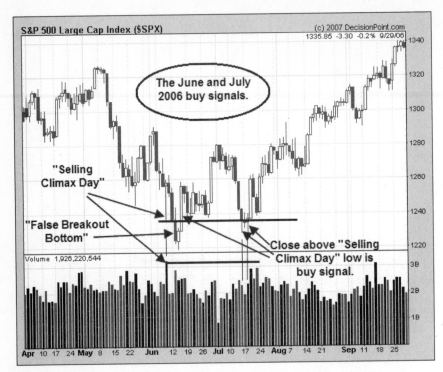

FIGURE 4.28   Selling Climax Day in June and July 2006 for S&P 500
Source: Chart courtesy of DecisionPoint.com.

2006, which was more than a 20 percent increase in volume compared to the days before June 8. The spike in volume on June 8 stands out noticeably and is a red-flag warning that the market was probably making a low. For the next two days after June 8 the market did work lower, but volume shrank significantly compared to June 8, showing that downside energy had dissipated and generating a bullish sign.

Notice in Figure 4.28 that when the June 8 low was broken, volume was very low compared to the June 8 volume and suggested a false break to the downside, which was a bullish condition. On June 15, the S&P 500 closed above the June 8 low, triggering a buy signal. A couple of more retests of the June 8 low followed in mid-July on lighter volume and also closed above the June 8 low, triggering additional buy signals. The rally that followed for the S&P 500 lasted into February 2007—eight months later. This event was a very good "wind at your back" trade for the S&P 500 index.

I might add that the Selling Climax Day works on all time frames. The next example is the Selling Climax on a weekly time frame for the NYSE

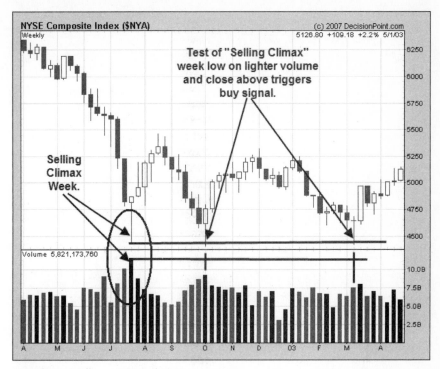

FIGURE 4.29 Selling Climax on a Weekly Chart of the NYSE Shows Buy Signals Triggered on Tests with Lighter Volume
Source: Chart courtesy of DecisionPoint.com.

at a major low in 2002, which is illustrated in Figure 4.29. The same rules apply for the weekly as for the daily. Here, the Selling Climax is marked by unusually high volume. Tests of the Selling Climax weekly low on lighter volume, with higher closes, triggered buy signals.

As you can see from the rules and examples illustrated in this chapter, volume plays a major role in determining price direction. In all cases, the trades to make are those in which the overall market is moving in the same direction, and you are picking stocks in the best sectors. These are truly the conditions to put the "wind at your back" as you trade.

In the next chapter, we will combine Chapter 3 Ord-Volume methods with the swing volume rules of Chapter 4 to get double volume confirmation of signals to achieve even higher probability of successful winning trades.

CHAPTER 5

Combining Ord-Volume with Swing Price and Volume Relationships

In the previous chapter, we discussed price and volume relationships—specifically how analysis of volume at swing points can predict whether the market has enough strength to pass through a previous swing or if it will reverse. Now in this chapter, we will combine Ord-Volume with price and volume relationships to give traders a clearer view of what the markets are trying to tell them.

Just to refresh: A *swing* is where an issue changes direction, and a *leg* is the distance between two swings. The Ord-Volume method is based on the average daily volume in a leg, which shows how much "energy" is in a particular leg. By comparing Ord-Volume from one leg to another, traders can identify which way the market energy is pushing.

As mentioned in previous chapters, my work is based on the methods developed by Richard Wyckoff, a master trader of the 1930s. Over the years, his methods have given me insight into volume analysis; for example, to confirm an uptrend, the stock should produce what he called a "Sign of Strength" as the stock rallies through the previous high. A Sign of Strength is a wide bullish spread and big volume. When a stock rallies through the previous highs with a Sign of Strength, he called this pattern "Jumping the Creek" (see Chapter 4).

In my analysis, I have taken Wyckoff's patterns and broken them down into smaller pieces to provide additional insight. These insights have led me to develop criteria for identifying trades with a higher probability of success and, therefore, lower risk.

For example, one of my rules is that when a stock rallies and tests its previous highs, volume should be near equal or greater than that of the previous high in order to exceed that level. However, if volume on the retest of the previous high shrinks by 8 percent or greater, then strength is not adequate to get through the old highs, and the market should reverse.

Therefore, the market can do one of two things on a test of previous highs or lows, as determined by the volume analysis (comparison of Ord-Volume):

- If volume is near equal or greater, it implies that the current rally has strength to head higher—which Wyckoff called "Jumping the Creek."
- If volume is lacking (declining by 8 percent or greater), then the previous high will turn into resistance and the market reverses. When the market turns back down, the next price target will be the previous low.

The same rules apply on the downside when a stock breaks its previous lows. Wyckoff also had names for weakness to the downside, which he called "Signs of Weakness." The Signs of Weakness are a wide price spread and big volume to the downside. When a stock breaks its previous low with a Sign of Weakness, he named this pattern "Falling through the Ice" (see Chapter 4).

All investment decisions are made at previous high or low swings. A trade should not be taken in the middle of a trading range. Rather, traders should wait to see the stock's volume as previous lows or previous highs are retested. The swings are the place to watch for trade setups, as these are the areas where risk is lowest and profit potential is highest.

Through volume analysis, traders will be able to read what the stock action is telling them. Always remember to "put the wind at your back" and select two or three best-performing sectors and select stocks in those sectors. (Index and sectors analysis will be covered in Chapter 6.) If you follow the rules, profitable trading should become much easier.

COMBINING ORD-VOLUME AND VOLUME RELATIONSHIPS

Volume analyses work on any price stock, whether it's a $1 issue or a $500 issue. What matters most is the not the price, but rather the volume of the issue. The higher the volume in the issue, the clearer the picture becomes using volume analysis. Traders sometimes shy away from low-priced stocks because they believe there is less safety. I differ in that view; in fact, I have made upwards of 10 times my investment in low-priced issues and continue to trade them.

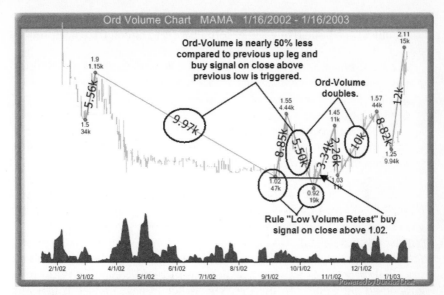

FIGURE 5.1   Ord-Volume Chart of Mamma.com Inc. (MAMA) Shows Relationships between Price Swings and Volume

Volume swings in lower-priced issues are often more easily identified than in higher-priced stocks, and they are more apt to generate clearer signals than higher-priced issues. That is not to imply that you should stay away from higher-priced issues. Trade whatever priced issue that you see fit, but make sure it has high activity (volume).

Figure 5.1 is a chart of Mamma.com Inc. (MAMA) in the Ord-Volume format, showing the swing point prices as well as the volumes at these points. This enables traders to identify trade setups based on price and volume relationships. The Ord-Volume charts help to identify the physics of price and volume (i.e., the magnitude of the volume "force" that is pushing the stock) as well as swing price and volume relationships. These two factors together will give the trader more confidence in the signals generated.

Ord-Volume Buy Signals

Looking at Figure 5.1, the leg down to the September 2002 low of $1.02 has Ord-Volume (average daily volume) of 9,700 (9.7k). MAMA bounced up to $1.55 a share and came down again, putting in a new low of $0.92 on volume of 5,000 (5.0k). The Ord-Volume on the move to a new low was nearly

50 percent less the previous leg and meets our bullish setup. Let's review for a moment the bullish buy signal setup for Ord-Volume from Chapter 3:

> *A buy signal is triggered when a stock hits a minor new low and Ord-Volume on the down leg shrinks by approximately 50 percent or greater against the previous down leg or previous up leg; the stock then closes above the previous low. Both conditions indicate the stock is in a strong position. Confirmation of a bottom is produced when Ord-Volume increases by 50 percent or more on the up leg after the bottom compared to the down leg going into the bottom.*

MAMA's close above the previous low of $1.02 triggered the Ord-Volume buy signal. As stated in the rule, we like to see Ord-Volume increase by 50 percent or more on the up leg after the buy signal is triggered to confirm the buy signal and show that energy has switched from down to up. In this example, Ord-Volume on the up leg after the buy signal came in at 3,400 (3.4k). This was not a 50 percent increase compared to the previous down leg going into the low, which would have caused traders to have doubts about the trade. However, on the next rise, Ord-Volume basically doubled to 10,000 (10k), which confirmed the buy signal.

As we can see in Figure 5.1, a "Low Volume Retest" (as discussed in Chapter 4) was created in MAMA at the September and October lows. A price low on MAMA formed at $1.02 on Ord-Volume of 47,000 (47k) in early September 2002. The market bounced and came down again, hitting a low of $0.92 on Ord-Volume of 19,000 (19k) in early November 2002. Volume shrank by 60 percent on the second low compared to the first low, showing that force to the downside on second low was very weak. A close above the first low of $1.02 triggered the buy signal.

Two different volume methods demonstrated in this example depicted buy signals being triggered in the same place. MAMA goes on to rally for the next two years and eventually hits a high of $17.49 a share.

Figure 5.2 shows Questar Corporation (STR) (which in Chapter 4 is displayed as Figure 4.15). STR generated a "Low Volume Retest" buy signal in mid-March 2006. The Low Volume Retest buy signal setup was pretty straightforward: In mid-March. STR tested a previous low on 75 percent reduced volume and closed above the previous low of $68 to generate the buy signal.

Figure 5.3 shows STR in the same time period in Ord-Volume format. Going into the $67.37 low of mid-March, Ord-Volume declined by 65 percent compared to the previous down leg, showing significantly less energy and indicating a bullish sign. A close above the previous low of $68 triggered the buy signal. On the next leg up after the buy signal, Ord-Volume of 57 million is only a 14 percent expansion compared to the previous down leg going into the low. As I've stated, we like to see an increase in volume of 50 percent or more on the rally leg after the buy signal

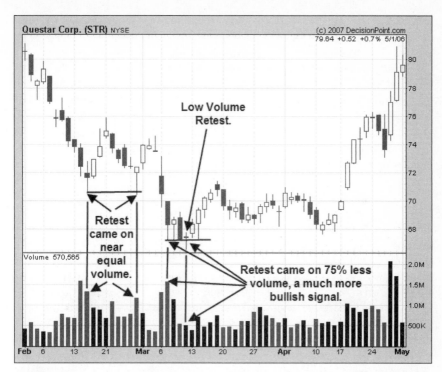

FIGURE 5.2   "Low Volume Retest" in Questar Corporation (STR) Generates Buy Signal
Source: Chart courtesy of DecisionPoint.com.

compared to the previous down leg going into the low. Therefore, this buy signal was not ideal.

The rally leg after the buy signal did show some strength (the 14 percent increase), and therefore it is promising. However, since true rally leg strength did not come in after the buy signal, STR languished in a trading range for a month. Notice in this trading range in Figure 5.3 that the up legs had more strength than the down legs, which suggested that the eventual breakout would be to the upside. STR did break to the upside in early April and Ord-Volume expanded by 50 percent compared to the previous down leg, and showed energy had definitely switched to the upside.

Ord-Volume Sell Signals

Before we go further let's review the sell signal set for the Ord-Volume method from Chapter 3:

A sell signal is triggered when a stock hits a minor new high and the Ord-Volume on the current up leg shrinks by approximately

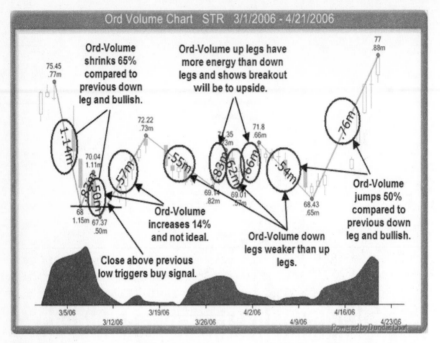

FIGURE 5.3   Ord-Volume Chart for Questar Corporation (STR) Shows Buy Signal Generated after Mid-March Low, but Volume on the Next Up Leg Is Not Ideal

50 percent or greater compared with the Ord-Volume of the previous up leg or down leg; the stock then closes below the previous high. Both conditions determine the stock is in a weak position. This triggers the sell signal. Confirmation of a top is produced when Ord-Volume increases by 50 percent or more on the down leg after the top compared to the up leg going into the top.

Figure 5.4 shows a sell signal triggered in JP Morgan Chase (JPM) in February 2007 (as seen in Figure 4.21 in Chapter 4). The selling signal trading pattern was called "False Breakout Top." In general, the False Breakout Top was a lighter-volume break above the late January 2007 highs. A close below the late January 2007 high triggered the sell signal.

Now let's compare that sell signal to Ord-Volume signal generated in the same time frame, using Figure 5.5, which shows the stock in Ord-Volume format. A lot of information can be derived from this chart view in Ord-Volume format. To start, let's compare the rally legs on JPM from the January 2007 low as it progressed into the high of mid-February 2007 and then the down leg thereafter.

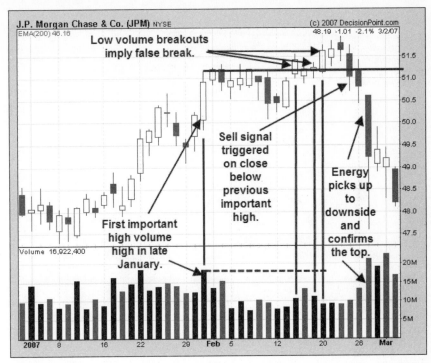

FIGURE 5.4 False Breakout Top Pattern Generated a Sell Signal in JP Morgan Chase (JPM)

Source: Chart courtesy of DecisionPoint.com.

The rally leg into the $50.68 high had Ord-Volume of 14 million compared to the previous up leg of 11 million, which showed that upside energy was increasing, the tone was bullish, and the rally should continue. The next rally leg into the $51.33 had Ord-Volume of 14 million, which was also a good comparison. It showed energy was steady, although not increasing compared to the previous up leg to $50.68; still, it was bullish and implied the rally should continue. When JPM rallied to $51.95, however, Ord-Volume shrank to 9.9 million, which was 30 percent less than the previous up leg and showed that energy had decreased by nearly a third. This was a bearish sign.

In the Ord-Volume definition of a sell signal, we like to see a 50 percent decrease in Ord-Volume in the rally leg into the top compared to the previous up leg or down leg. A 50 percent decrease in Ord-Volume on the final leg up compared to the previous up leg or down leg is a stronger sell setup than a stock that has a 30 percent decrease in Ord-Volume on

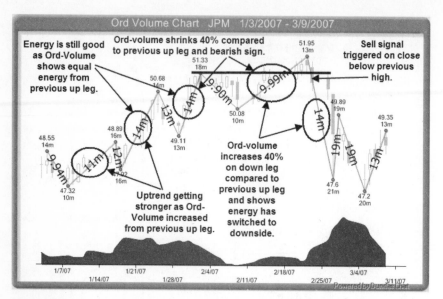

FIGURE 5.5   Ord-Volume Chart Format Shows Detail of Volume Comparisons at Key Price Points in JP Morgan Chase (JPM)

the final leg into the top. Therefore, if a trader had a choice between two stocks to sell short—one with a 50 percent shrinkage and the other a 30 percent shrinkage in Ord-Volume compared to the previous up leg or down leg—the trader would take the one with the stronger sell signal and the greater decline (50 percent) in Ord-Volume.

Going back to our example of JPM, notice that on the down leg from the $51.95 high that Ord-Volume increased by 40 percent to 14.0 million compared to the previous up leg (9.9 million), which showed that energy had switched from the upside to the downside. This confirmed the bearish signal.

Although we like to see a 50 percent increase in Ord-Volume on the down leg after the sell signal compared to the previous up leg, and a 40 percent increase in down leg volume was not as strong a confirmation as we would have liked, the trade did work fine. In situations such as these, it's up to traders to define their degree of safety in trading signals. Using the Ord-Volume format, a trader can judge the degree of safety. I have found that a 50 percent shrinkage in Ord-Volume at the final highs or lows works well for us. Keep in mind that all signals are to be taken in the direction of the overall market, and traders should pick stocks in the best sectors. (Market direction trend signals and sector trend signals will be covered in Chapters 6 and 7.)

UNDERSTANDING VOLUME PUSHING PRICE AND TIME FRAMES

In this section, we will discuss two important concepts. The first is how volume pushes price; it is the fuel that moves an issue upward or downward. Therefore, volume, not price, is the most important factor. The second is to look at a stock in a larger time frame in order to comprehend its "bigger picture," before analyzing the buy and sell trade setups that appear in the shorter time frames.

Volume and Price Direction

As previously stated, volume plays a very important role in defining price direction. Here is a visual representation to prove this point. Figure 5.6 is an Ord-Volume chart of Eldorado Gold Corporation (EGO) with a long-term view: dating back to where this stock started trading in early 2003. We have recorded the "impulse waves" that showed a steady increase in Ord-Volume. Notice that each impulse wave upward had higher Ord-Volume

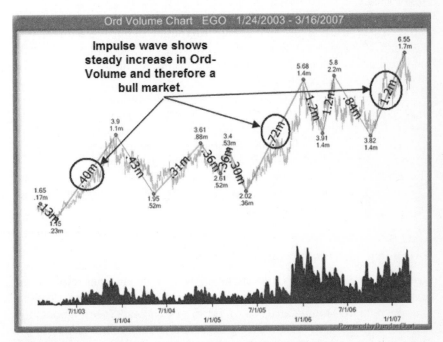

FIGURE 5.6   Ord-Volume Chart of Eldorado Gold (EGO) Shows Steady Increase in the Ord-Volume of Impulse Waves, Moving the Stock Price Higher

values than the previous impulse wave. For a rally to continue, Ord-Volume on the current impulse wave needs to be at least equal or higher then the previous impulse wave.

Figure 5.6 of EGO also shows impressive percentage gains on each Ord-Volume impulse wave upward, starting in early 2003, which implied that this stock would continue to rally as energy was increasing on each new impulse wave up. This shows visually that volume pushes price. These are the conditions that make bull markets.

Once Ord-Volume decreases as a market breaks to new highs, then the rally phase will be coming to an end. Volume is like fuel to push the rally higher, and when volume decreases as the market is hitting new highs that energy is being taken away from the rally and the rally will end. Since volume pushes price, when volume is absent, the price does not move.

Time Frames and the "Bigger Picture"

When evaluating a particular stock, it's important to look at the bigger trend first and compare volume in the impulse waves for a two- or three-year period. If Ord-Volume has been expanding on the major impulse waves then it is safe to assume that an issue is in a major bull move, and traders would look to buy on bullish setups as described in Chapters 3 and 4. When an issue has increasing Ord-Volume impulse wave then you are putting "the wind at your back" on the bigger time frame, which will help push the stock higher in the shorter-term time frames. This, in term, gives bullish setups higher success.

It is important to understand that the longer-term time frames (the "bigger picture") rule the shorter time frames. The goal is to align your shorter-term trading to the overall direction of the longer term. This way, you will have the forces within the longer time frame pushing your stock in your favor—as well as the dynamics of the shorter-term time frames. This combination makes for successful trading. Therefore, keep "the wind at your back" on the longer-term time frames to help build successful trading in the shorter-term time frames.

Swing Prices, Volume, and Ord-Volume

Moving on, let's compare Ord-Volume analysis to swing price and volume analysis, this time using the example of Novamerican Steel, Inc. (TONS). We covered Ord-Volume analysis of TONS in Chapter 3 (see Figure 3.16), but let's look again in light of swing price and volume relationships to the Ord-Volume method. My goal is to show that volume analysis does give important information of what to expect in the price action of an issue.

FIGURE 5.7   Candlestick Chart of Novamerican Steel (TONS) Shows that Volume Is Declining as Rally Continues, Indicating a Top Is Near
Source: Chart courtesy of DecisionPoint.com.

In Figure 5.7, which is a candlestick chart of TONS, we can see a decline in volume as the rally continued, indicating that a top was approaching. Observation of the volume in TONS could have helped to identify the approaching top near $90. Notice in this figure how from January to late February 2005, volume gradually decreased as TONS rallied. This demonstrated that upside energy was subsiding. With the reduction in "fuel" to push the market higher, this stock was doomed to reverse.

It is much easier to see the volume contraction and determine the leg volume relationship when using the Ord-Volume format. With a trained eye, traders can use this format to make general estimates in volume comparisons. In Figure 5.8, TONS is displayed in a monthly format to depict more clearly the significant decrease in volume (energy) in February 2005 as TONS rallied to the $90 high. After the high at the $90 level, notice the

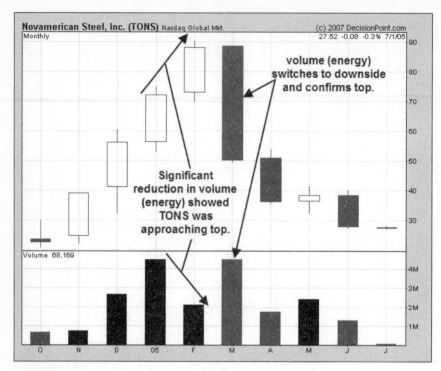

FIGURE 5.8 Ord-Volume Chart Shows Significant Reduction in Volume as Novamerican Steel TONS Approaches the Top in February 2005
Source: Chart courtesy of DecisionPoint.com.

large increase in volume in March as the stock traded lower, which confirmed the top and showed energy had switched to the downside.

Figure 5.9 shows TONS in the same time frame but from a different perspective, using the swing price and volume relationship to trigger a sell signal. (This setup was discussed in Chapter 4, Figure 4.20, as a "False Breakout.") The signature of this pattern is when an issue breaks to a new high and volume shrinks by 10 percent or more compared to that of the previous high. This condition shows energy is lacking on the breakout to the upside, and at some point the market will reverse back to the downside. The sell signal is triggered on the close below the previous high.

The monthly chart of TONS in Figure 5.9 indicates (see solid line on chart) that a close below the $75 level will trigger a sell signal. This sell setup would be nearly impossible to see on a daily chart; however, in a monthly chart it shows very clearly. My point is that if daily charts do not show any setups then switch to a weekly or monthly time frame—and sometimes a signal will jump out at you.

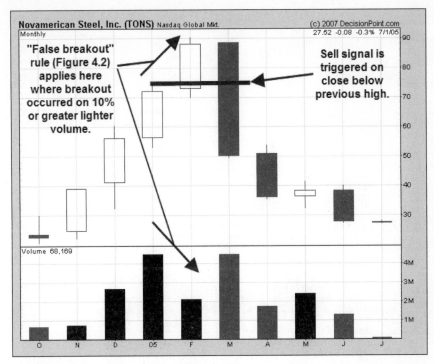

FIGURE 5.9   Ord-Volume Chart for TONS Shows "False Breakout" Rule and the Triggering of a Sell Signal with a Close below Previous High
Source: Chart courtesy of DecisionPoint.com.

Now let's take a look at TONS again in the Ord-Volume format in the same time frame in Figure 5.10. (We saw this view in Chapter 3, Figure 3.16.) Right away, you can see there is a problem going into the high at $90.27 because volume was 110,000 shares (0.11 m)—or 60 percent less than the Ord-Volume (average daily volume) of the previous up leg of 270,000 (0.27 m). As previously stated, when Ord-Volume shrinks by 50 percent or more compared to the previous up leg or down leg, then a reversal in the market is about to occur. A close below the previous high (in this case a close below $74.85) triggers the sell signal.

Now notice the Ord-Volume for the down leg after the high at $90.27, which is double at 220,000 shares (0.22 m) compared to the previous up leg. This confirms the top. Although the sell signals triggered for TONS by Ord-Volume and swing price and volume methods came in at the same levels, both methods used volume in different ways to achieve the same outcome. Both methods looked for decreased energy as the market broke out—one

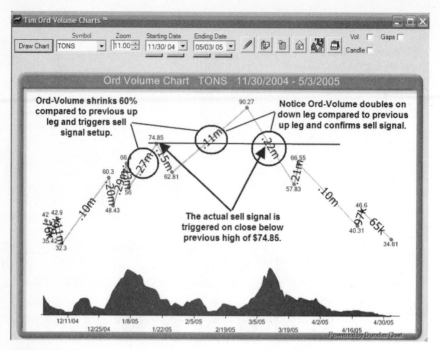

FIGURE 5.10 Ord-Volume Analysis of Novamerican Steel (TONS) Shows 60 Percent Decline in Volume in Up Leg to High at $90.27, Indicating a Market Reversal Is Near

method by price swings and volume analysis and the other by leg volume analysis.

The sell signal setup using swing price and volume analysis on a daily chart for TONS was nearly impossible to identify, although it become clearer when the view was switched to a monthly chart. In the monthly time frame, the Ord-Volume method sell signal setup was immediately visible. Both sell signals were successful, but the swing price and volume method took a little more research to identify.

Let's examine another stock that we have already looked at using Ord-Volume analysis: 8 × 8 Inc. (EGHT). (See Chapter 3, Figure 3.24.) To refresh, Figure 5.11 shows the bullish setup going into the low at $1.32 in August 2004, with volume of 290,000 shares (0.29m). Ord-Volume on the down leg to the $1.32 low was nearly 50 percent less than the Ord-Volume for the previous up leg of 570,000 (0.57m) as well as the Ord-Volume for the previous down leg of 680,000 (0.68m). This shrinkage in Ord-Volume

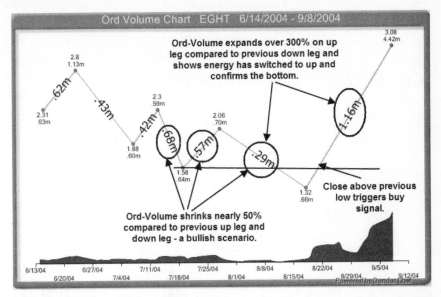

FIGURE 5.11   Ord-Volume Analysis for 8 × 8 Inc. (EGHT) Shows 50 Percent Decline in Ord-Volume on Down Leg Going into Low at $1.32, Setting Up a Bullish Condition

as the market hit new lows shows the down force was very weak, indicating a bullish condition was developing.

As Figure 5.11 shows, a buy signal is triggered on a close above the previous low of $1.58. Furthermore, the buy signal is confirmed by an expansion in Ord-Volume of over 300 percent on the up leg after the buy signal. This is pretty straightforward, with nothing left to the imagination. Still, let's look at EGHT using swing price and volume analysis to see if an additional confirmation could be found using this method.

Figure 5.12 is a candlestick chart of EGHT, marking the swing low from July 19, 2004, with lines drawn from that low as well as from the volume close. Then, as EGHT breaks the July 19 low, volume does not contract to a significant degree, which would have suggested that energy to the downside had dissipated—although not significantly, which would leave the trader with uncertainty.

As Figure 5.12 shows, EGHT did work lower and volume also picked up somewhat at the price lows. Therefore, using the swing price and volume method on a daily chart of EGHT alone, mostly likely a trade would *not* have been taken at the price low. However, look at what happens after EGHT comes off its low in mid-August 2004: Volume picks up substantially as the stock hits the previous high from late July. The higher volume

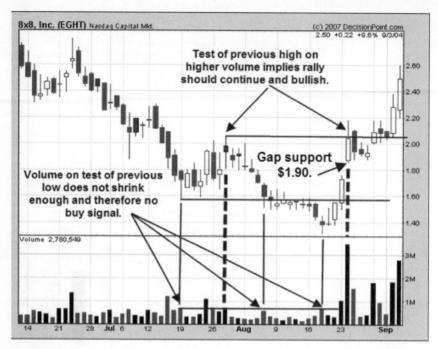

FIGURE 5.12   Candlestick Chart of 8 × 8 (EGHT) Shows Volume Does Not Decline Significantly after a Low Is Put in on July 19, 2004, Creating Uncertainty
Source: Chart courtesy of DecisionPoint.com.

on this upward move created a bullish "High Volume Retest." At this point, the scenario for this stock would be viewed as bullish and the outlook would be for it to move higher. Further, a gap formed nearly $1.90, which would have prompted a trader to initiate a long position near the gap level using the "Gap Test" rule as outlined in Chapter 4.

The important lesson here, though, is that the swing price and volume analysis method using a daily chart for EGHT would *not* have gotten the trader into the market with a long position near the price low, although it did confirm the bullish upswing after the price low.

Let's take another look at EGHT, this time using a weekly time frame and the swing price and volume method. In Figure 5.13, the weekly time frame for EGHT reveals a different conclusion using the swing price and volume analysis near the price low, compared to the daily chart. Using a weekly time frame, we can see that after the July 19 low, volume does contract as the stock works lower, which is a bullish setup. Further, a close above the previous swing low triggers a bullish signal.

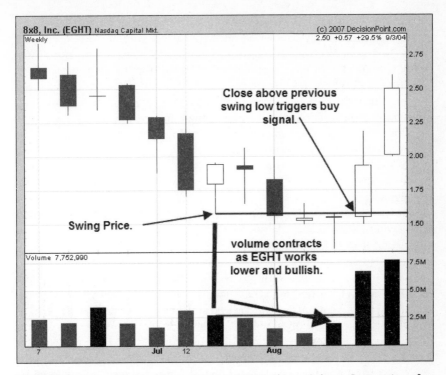

FIGURE 5.13   Weekly Chart of 8 × 8 (EGHT) Shows Volume Contracting after the July 19 Low, Indicating a Bullish Scenario
Source: Chart courtesy of DecisionPoint.com.

USING LONGER AND SHORTER CHART TIME FRAMES

The lesson here is to use different time frames to view an issue. When the longer-term time frames reveal an overall trend, then you can put the "wind at your back" as you trade the smaller time frames. This means that if the longer-term time frame reveals a bullish tone in a stock, then you will look for a trade setup in the shorter time frames to buy that stock and go long. This time frame comparison also holds true for signals that are generated on a daily and weekly basis.

As we've seen in these examples, a signal will have more importance on a weekly chart than a daily chart. Remember, the longer time frames rule the shorter ones. To review this time frame relationship using Figure 5.13, we can see that the swing low occurred in the third week of July

2004 at the $1.58 level. A couple of weeks later the market worked lower and broke the weekly low of $1.58 on reduced volume; this created a "False Breakout Bottom" (Chapter 4, Figure 4.22). To confirm the down-trend, volume should have matched or exceeded that of the previous low. (As you recall, Wyckoff called this confirmation of breaking to new lows "Falling through the Ice.") To get through the previous low, energy (volume) must be at least equal to or higher than the previous down leg.

However, as a stock breaks to a new low if the volume is at least 10 percent less, then the whole scenario changes to a bullish tone—which is the case of the weekly break to new lows in EGHT. The stock closed above the swing low of $1.58 in the fourth week of August, triggering a buy signal.

Now, with the weekly setup identified and confirmed, traders would have switched back to a daily chart to purchase EGHT where they felt most comfortable following a daily close above $1.58. If a trader waited for the close on a weekly time frame, the purchase price would have been near $1.90. On a daily basis, the $1.58 swing low was exceeded on August 23, 2004, with a recorded high that day of $1.76. Trading with a daily chart, therefore, a trader's entry point would not have exceeded $1.76 on that buy signal. (In other words, using a daily chart for a specific entry point for a long trade, the entry would have been no higher than $1.76, compared with $1.90 for the weekly chart.)

A couple of points should be emphasized here for clarity. Let's assume that the swing price and volume analysis gave a weekly time frame buy signal, but did not generate a buy signal on a daily time frame. Since the weekly time frame would rule over the daily, a trader would have taken the weekly buy signal. However, if the daily time frame had triggered a buy signal, but the weekly time frame did *not*, then a trader would have less confidence in that daily buy signal. If trader did take the daily buy signal, and the weekly time frame did not turn bullish, then it would be more of a "scalp trade" for a short-term, small profit, instead of a bigger potential "shooting for the moon" long-term trade.

In order to "shoot for the moon" for a bigger profit potential, a trader needs the weekly chart with its longer-term time frame to be in favor as well.

SUMMING IT UP: SWING PRICE, VOLUME, AND ORD-VOLUME

In Chapters 3, 4, and 5, I have explained how volume can be used in swing trades as well as in leg trades to trigger buy and sell signals. It may take traders a bit of time to wrap their minds around the new concepts about volume (energy); however, I believe they will discover—just as I have—that the volume concepts presented in this book will be a valuable tool to use in the stock market.

My hope is that traders feel increased confidence with this knowledge of volume analysis to help them identify strengths and weakness in stocks, helping them to attain their financial goals more quickly and with greater assurance.

CHAPTER 6

The "Wind at Your Back" Method

As we discussed in Chapter 2, investing requires a top-down approach comprised of three steps. The first step is to find the direction of the market in a three- to six-month time frame so that you can trade stocks in that direction. The second step is to find the best performing sectors that are aligned with the market. The third step is to find the strongest stocks in the best performing sectors.

The important lesson here is that even before you begin to look for stocks to invest in, you need to know whether the market is going in your direction and what the best performing sectors are. In this chapter, we are going to take an in-depth look at the first step—finding the direction of the market.

FINDING MARKET DIRECTION

Finding market direction involves its own three-step process: breadth analysis, volume analysis, and momentum analysis. When all three analyses line up in the same direction, you have put the odds in your favor. In other words, you have achieved the goal of putting the "wind at your back," which will help propel your investments in the desired direction.

This makes sense if you think about it: When the advance/decline ratio (which is the breadth of the market) is rising, you know that more issues are jumping onto the rally wagon. When volume increases, more demand is entering the market, pushing stocks higher. With momentum rising and stocks going higher, you would be hard pressed to find an issue going in the opposite direction. This is the time to be in the market.

When Investing Is Like Gambling

Many people believe that investing in the stock market is akin to gambling. The reason is that they do not have a rhyme or reason behind their investing. These investors open up the financial pages of the newspaper and scan the thousands of stocks listed, trying to pick out the ones they like. Or they go to the library or browse the Internet to research whatever fundamental facts they can find on a stock. That, to me, is gambling. For all they know, they could be buying a stock in a weak sector that's peaking or declining, or they could be buying at the time the whole market is peaking or in a downtrend. The only chance that these investors have to make money would be due to luck—or maybe because they unknowingly entered the market with the wind at their backs.

Let's say that these investors did get in at the right time and their stocks rallied significantly. What would happen when their stock sectors turned down along with the rest of the market because the overall direction has shifted? Now the wind is in their faces and not at their backs. Would these investors know it's time to sell?

The fundamentals on their stocks may not have changed and may even have improved. Still, the odds have turned against them because the overall market has shifted course. These investors, however, are caught totally unaware when their stocks head south. I have been there and done that, and I didn't like it a bit! Fortunately, I learned some valuable lessons about making sure the market direction was with me, not against me. I saw the need to determine the direction of the market first, identify two or three strong sectors that are moving in the same direction as the market, and then pick stocks in those sectors. Only after performing those three essential steps was there any need to look at the fundamentals of the stocks, although even then it's not necessary. The technical factors of a stock will carry it forward.

The Broader Markets

The markets I follow are the S&P 500 Large Cap Index (SPX), NYSE Composite Index (NYA), and Nasdaq Composite Index (COMPQ). I also follow gold issues, which I have been bullish on since early 2002. The indexes I monitor for gold issues are the S&P/TSX Capped Gold Index (SPTGD) and Market Vectors Gold Miners (GDX). I do watch the Gold and Silver Index (XAU) and Gold Bugs (HUI), but volume on these two indexes is not readily available, whereas volume plays an important role in my analysis of SPTGD and GDX.

BREADTH ANALYSIS

Breadth analysis measures the number of issues in an index that is advancing and the number that is declining. In a healthy market (one that is rising), most of the stocks will be advancing and stock leadership will be broad based. Tops are found in the market when stock leadership narrows, and fewer stocks are carrying the rally forward. The top comes when these last few stocks make their highs and turn downward.

For breadth analysis, I use the McClellan Oscillator and the McClellan Summation Index developed by Sherman and Marion McClellan back in the 1960s. The McClellan Oscillator and Summation Index have stood the test of time and are among the best indicators for determining strong or weak breadth. As I said in Chapter 2, the formula for the McClellan Oscillator is fairly complex. The simple explanation is that it is basically the result of subtracting a 39-day exponential average of advances minus declines (5 percent index) from a 19-day exponential average (10 percent index). The McClellan Summation Index is derived by adding together the previous day's McClellan Summation Index and the current day's McClellan Oscillator.

As explained earlier, I use the McClellan Oscillator and Summation Index as breadth indicators, using the New York Stock Exchange (NYSE) in order to get a good indication of where the market is at any given time. I prefer to use the Summation Index of the NYSE, instead of the S&P 500, because the Summation Index for the NYSE has smoother runs from high to low and low to high, and also has less volatility. Therefore, it produces clearer signals. I use the Nasdaq Composite Index instead of the Nasdaq 100 Index for McClellan Oscillator and Summation Index analyses because the Nasdaq Composite also has less volatility and produces clearer signals.

The NYSE and Nasdaq Composite have more issues in them compared to S&P 500 and Nasdaq 100, respectively, which is why the McClellan Oscillator and Summation Index have smoother patterns. The reason why the McClellan Oscillator and Summation Index are such good indicators of breadth is that they oscillates from high to low and low to high, allowing traders to set boundaries for overbought and oversold levels. The McClellan Oscillator can be used to identify short-term overbought and oversold levels, as well as to identify capitulation in the market where bottoms start to form. The Summation Index can be used to identify longer-term highs and lows and can find trends in the market that last usually three to six months. The Summation Index is derived by adding today's Oscillator reading to yesterday's Summation Index reading, which yields today's Summation Index reading.

Summation Index Signals

Since our time frame encompasses three- to six-month swings, most of our attention will be on the McClellan Summation Index. In Chapter 2, I explained that when the NYSE Summation Index trades above +3,500 and then closes below +3,500, it is a "shot over the bow" or a warning signal that the NYSE may be nearing a top. In general, that condition will indicate a topping process has begun when used in conjunction with the other two filters of volume and momentum. In other words when the NYSE Summation Index has turned downward from over the +3500 level, volume has triggered bearish signs as well, and momentum (as measured by the weekly moving average convergence/divergence [MACD] or Price Momentum Oscillator [PMO] indicators) has also turned down, then conditions in all three analyses have been met and a downtrend may be underway. In this chapter, I will give further details for buy and sell signals generated by analysis of breadth, volume, and momentum.

In the years to come, the overbought and oversold levels for the Summation Index may change, but that should happen gradually, allowing us to make accurate adjustments. Figure 6.1 shows the McClellan Oscillator and Summation Index for the NYSE dating back to 1996. It shows the boundary lines over overbought and oversold levels for the NYSE Summation Index in different time frames.

Figure 6.2 shows that, in general (starting in 1996 and ending mid-2007), the NYSE was approaching a high when the Summation Index was greater than +3,000 and, in general, it was approaching a low when the Summation Index was below −500.

In Figure 6.3, going back to 1996, I have identified the areas where capitulation in the NYSE occurs when the McClellan Oscillator records readings below −230. Readings below −230 on the McClellan Oscillator predict the market is at extreme oversold levels, which is the type of condition that appears near intermediate-term bottoms. The McClellan Oscillator reading below −230 is the first sign the NYSE is approaching a low. Bear market will not achieve a McClellan Oscillator reading below −230. The −230 (preferable lower) reading on the McClellan Oscillator shows capitulation which is the condition that appears at bottoms. As more issues are added to the NYSE in the coming years, the advance/decline line will have higher and lower extremes and increase the capitulation level of the McClellan Oscillator. Right now McClellan Oscillator readings below −230 is and indication the NYSE is near a bottom.

Notice in early 2007 that the McClellan Oscillator hit below −300 and predicted a bottom, while the McClellan Summation Index was at an overbought level near +4,000. It is said that an overbought market can last longer than a trader who is short the market can remain solvent. Here, the

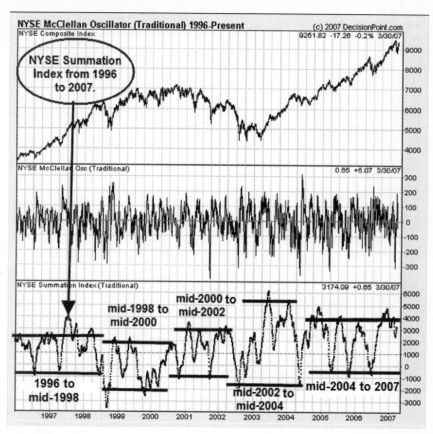

FIGURE 6.1 McClellan Oscillator and Summation Index for NYSE from 1996 through Q1 2007
Source: Chart courtesy of DecisionPoint.com.

McClellan Oscillator reached a climatic low below −230, which predicted an intermediate-term significant low. This condition implied that the McClellan Summation Index would remain overbought for a while longer.

Remember, there are no absolutes in technical analysis, only probabilities. Once the McClellan Oscillator hits below −230 to indicate the NYSE has hit capitulation, to confirm a bottom in the NYSE, the McClellan Oscillator should switch immediately and rally to +175 or higher to show that the advance/decline line has switched from down to up. This two-step process on the McClellan Oscillator can be found at all significant lows on the NYSE. After the McClellan Oscillator reaches past +175 to confirm a bottom, the NYSE can pull back and test the previous low (like it did in

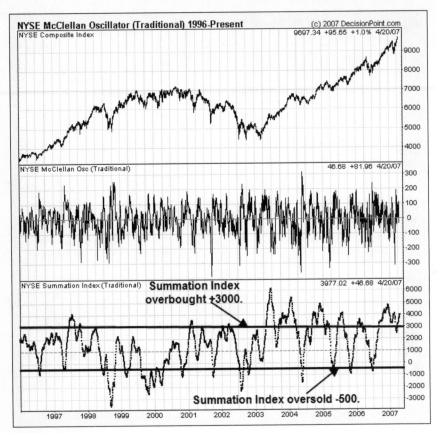

FIGURE 6.2 McClellan Oscillator and Summation Index for NYSE, with Summation Index Showing Overbought Conditions above +3,000 and Oversold below −500
Source: Chart courtesy of DecisionPoint.com.

mid-2004) or stall in a sideways pattern for a short while then work higher (like in mid-2007). What is important in determining a bottom in the NYSE is that first the McClellan Oscillator must reach capitulation with a read below −230 and then hit +175 or higher to show strength in the advance/ decline line and confirm the bottom. I might add that McClellan Oscillator readings much lower then −230 (say near −350 or lower) imply a greater degree of capitulation and therefore a larger degree bottom (and therefore expect a longer lasting rally). Also the McClellan Oscillator reading after the capitulation reading that reaches past +200 imply the coming rally will be much stronger than if the McClellan Oscillator reached just +175 range. In Figure 6.4, I pointed out these instances—where the McClellan

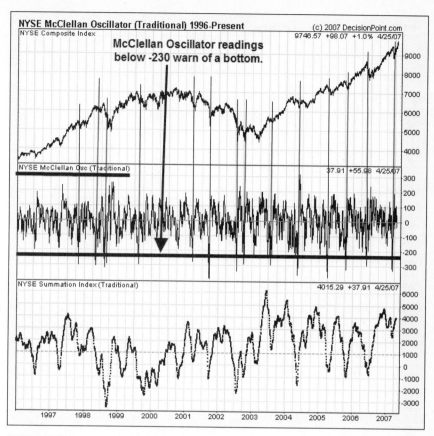

FIGURE 6.3 McClellan Oscillator Shows Readings below −230, Which Indicate Oversold Conditions and Predict a Bottom
Source: Chart courtesy of DecisionPoint.com.

Oscillator went below −230 and then rose to above +175 to confirm a bottom—going back to 2004. This chart also shows the oscillator reading touching below −300 and then reaching near +200 in early 2007 and predicted the rally that followed.

Figure 6.5 is the NYSE Index, showing the McClellan Oscillator and Summation Index from January 2004 through April 2007. The boundary for the NYSE Summation Index changed in that time frame to an overbought level of +3500 and to an oversold level of below −500. Since 2004, the first sign of trouble in the market is when the Summation Index traded above +3,500 and then closed below +3,500. This condition is a "shot over the bow" as the advance/decline line is starting to contract as

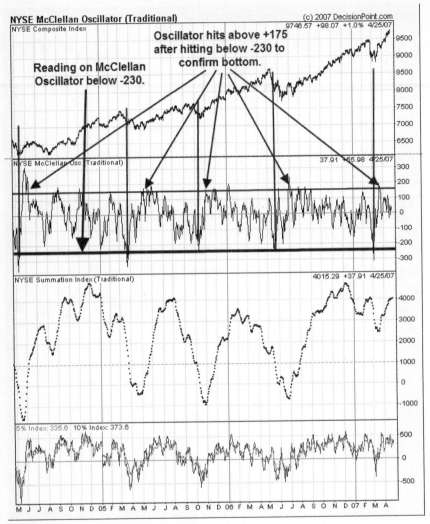

FIGURE 6.4   McClellan Oscillator Readings below −230 to Indicate Oversold and Then above +175 to Confirm a Bottom
Source: Chart courtesy of DecisionPoint.com.

the market is moving higher, which is a bearish condition. This shows that there are now fewer stocks carrying the rally higher.

Since 2004, when the NYSE Summation Index turned down from +3,500, the subsequent high was lower, while the NYSE made a higher high, which showed fewer stocks were carrying the rally and created a negative divergence.

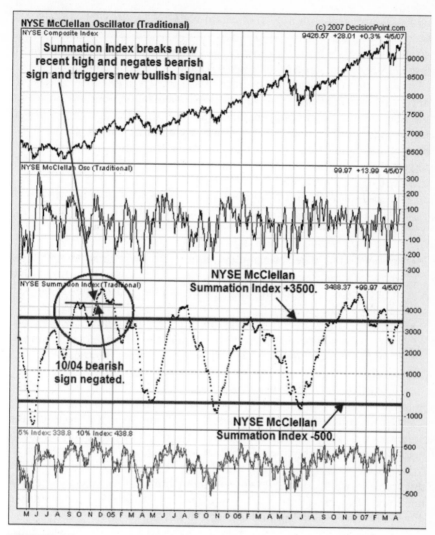

FIGURE 6.5   NYSE McClellan Oscillator for 2004 through April 2007
Source: Chart courtesy of DecisionPoint.com.

The NYSE McClellan Summation Index also helps you to identify when conditions, which once were bearish, have turned back to bullish. Direct your attention in Figure 6.5 to the area dated October 2004. At that time, the Summation Index had turned down from a high of over +4000 and closed below +3,500, which was a bearish sign. Then, in early November 2004, the Summation Index turned back up, hitting a higher high above its previous high of +4,000 along with the NYSE. This showed that the Summation Index had found new energy as the advance/decline line strengthened and broke to new recent highs—thus showing that more issues were carrying the rally forward. This was a bullish condition.

Once the Summation Index turns down from a high above +3,500, to keep the bearish scenario the Summation Index should not trade above its previous high in the topping episode. If it does, then the uptrend has been renewed and the market (NYSE) should head higher. Likewise, when the Summation Index turns down from above +3,500 and the NYSE makes higher highs and the Summation Index makes lower highs than the previous high, the bearish scenario is reinforced.

When the NYSE McClellan Summation Index turns down from above +3,500, it is a "shot over the bow." What comes after that warning sign is a sell signal setup for the NYSE Summation Index, as follows:

- The second high on the Summation Index is lower than the first high, and the NYSE has made a higher high. This condition shows that fewer issues are carrying the market higher and creates a bearish breadth divergence.
- The second low of the Summation Index trades below the first low, which shows the downward momentum in the advance/decline line).
- The Summation Index turns down again, triggering the sell signal.

Figure 6.6 for NYSE shows sell signals since 2004. In all cases the Summation Index produced a "shot over the bow" warning sign that started the sell-signal setup process. I have numbered the tops on the Summation Index as "1" and "2," indicating where the Summation Index made lower highs—the first step of the sell-signal process. I numbered as "3" the point on the Summation Index where the second low is lower than the first low, which shows downward momentum on the advance/decline line. Next, I marked with an arrow where the Summation Index turned down after the second low and triggered a sell signal.

As you can see, this method did a good job of identifying where and when weakness was entering the market and triggering sell signals that were either at the top or close to it. Notice in Figure 6.6 that in April 2007 all three requirements were met for a sell signal triggered by the NYSE Summation Index: The Summation Index reached the overbought level of +3,500; the NYSE made higher highs while the Summation Index put in lower highs, creating a bearish divergence; and the second low in the Summation Index was lower than the first low, which showed downside momentum in the advance/decline line and a bearish condition. The Summation Index would need to turn down to complete the sell signal.

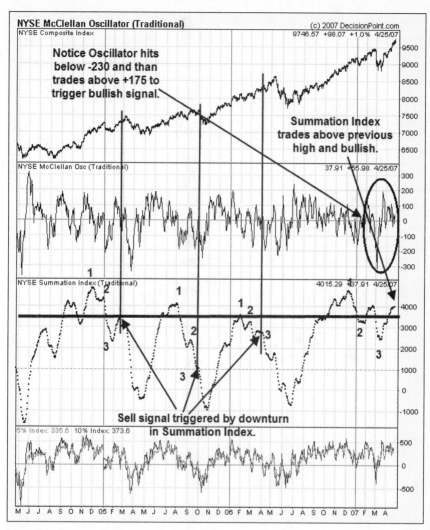

FIGURE 6.6   NYSE McClellan Oscillator, Marked with Significant Tops (1 and 2),
Lower Second low (3), and Triggering of Sell Signal (arrow)
Source: Chart courtesy of DecisionPoint.com.

However, the Summation Index in late April traded above the previous
high and triggered a *bullish* signal, negating the bearish setup. Also notice
that the McClellan Oscillator hit below −230 and then traded above
+175 to trigger a bullish signal. As I have said, tops usually take longer to
develop and take more study to identify.

Using the Summation Index to Pick Bottoms

Bottoms, however, are a bit easier to identify using the Summation Index, and take a shorter time frame to develop. Let's look at how the McClellan Summation Index can pick out bottoms in the NYSE. Figure 6.7 shows the NYSE and its McClellan Oscillator and Summation Index dating back to 1996. This chart illustrates what the levels at which the McClellan Summation Index bottoms out to pick lows in the NYSE.

Since 1996, the NYSE has reached a bottom at the same time that the Summation Index gone down to just below −500. This has occurred nine times since 1996. In this time frame, the NYSE reached a bottom three times when the Summation Index fell to below −2,000. Therefore, when the NYSE McClellan Summation Index goes below −500, a trader

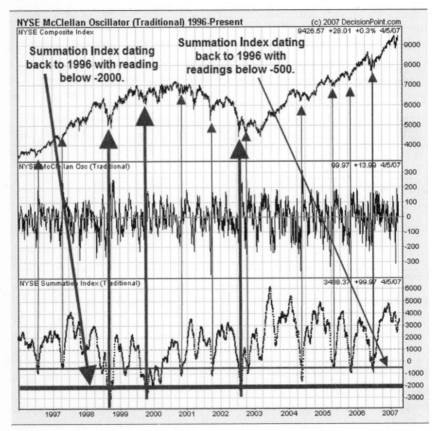

FIGURE 6.7   Summation Index Setups for Picking Bottoms in NYSE from 1996 through Q1 2007
Source: Chart courtesy of DecisionPoint.com.

would be advised to start looking for a low. It's not a bottom, however, until the Summation Index turns up from below −500. Therefore, if the Summation Index keeps going down below −500, then the trend in the market is still downward. The Summation Index could go as low as −750 or lower before it turns up.

Notice in Figure 6.8 the May 2004 time frame when the NYSE Summation index fell to nearly −1,500 before turning up. The NYSE did bottom

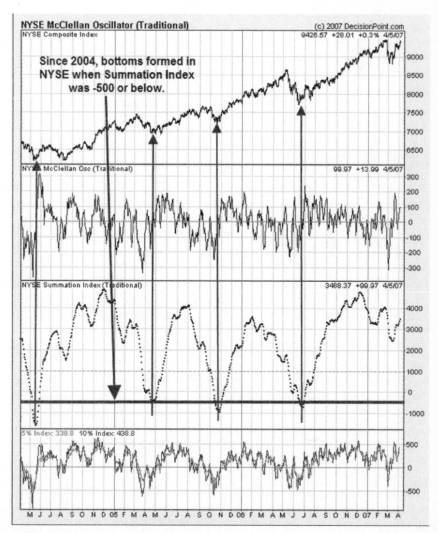

FIGURE 6.8 Summation Index Shows Drop to Nearly −1,500 in May 2004 and a Retest of That Low Again in August 2004
Source: Chart courtesy of DecisionPoint.com.

out when the Summation Index was near the −1,500 level, but the market did test that low again in August 2004 as the Summation Index made a much higher low. This condition showed that the August 2004 low was stronger because more issues were carrying the rally off that low compared to the May low.

To pick a bottom in the NYSE with the Summation Index, the first condition is that the index must be at an extremely oversold level of −500 or lower to indicate capitulation in the market. As Figure 6.9 shows, no signal is generated until the Summation Index turns up from below −500. Once the Summation Index turns back up from below −500, this shows that the advance/decline line is now improving, and more issues are starting to carry the rally. This is a bullish condition. As you can see, this process of picking bottoms using the NYSE Summation Index is much easier and quicker than identifying tops with the Summation Index.

VOLUME ANALYSIS

After breadth analysis, the second step in determining "the wind at your back" is volume analysis. Remembering, all three analyses—breadth, volume, and momentum, must line up in the same direction in order to have the wind at your back and reduce your risk for putting your money in the market.

In Chapters 3, 4 and 5, we covered volume analysis for equities in detail. Now we will cover volume analysis for the indexes, which is similar to the process we used for equities. In previous chapters, I stressed that volume is the force behind stocks. The same applies to the indexes. Volume pushes the indexes up or down, and the market goes in the direction of the legs with the highest volume.

Because we are dealing with the longer-term time frame of trends that last three to six months, weekly charts of the indexes provide the best picture for this time frame. I have also found that the S&P 500 SPDRs (SPY) and PowerShares QQQ Trust (QQQQ) for the Nasdaq Global Market have higher volume differences than the S&P 500 (SPX) and Nasdaq Composite (COMPQ), and therefore are easier to identify energy directional changes. Our volume studies of the indexes will be use SPY and QQQQ to represent the S&P 500 and Nasdaq Composite.

Tops form in markets because energy to the upside has run out. Volume is energy; therefore, when a market hits new highs and volume shrinks, the rally is doomed to fail. To do volume comparisons, we look at previous weekly highs in the market and compare volume as those highs are being tested. On the test, we look to see if volume is equal to or greater than the volume of the previous high to determine if the rally has

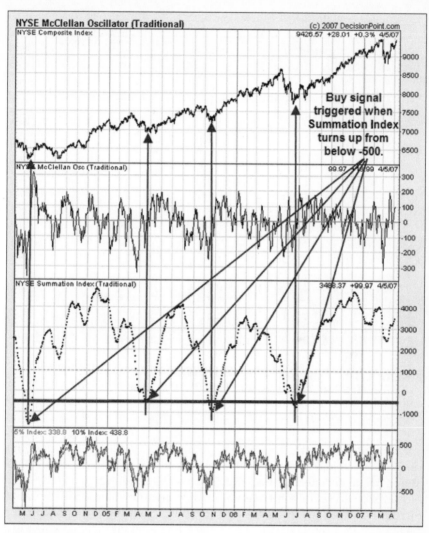

FIGURE 6.9   Buy Signals Are Triggered when the Summation Index Turns Up
from Below −500
Source: Chart courtesy of DecisionPoint.com.

energy to pass through the highs, or if volume is at least 10 percent less,
which means the highs will be rejected. This can be seen most clearly
using longer time frames and weekly charts.

Figure 6.10 is a weekly chart of SPY from December 2003 through
August 2004. Notice that as SPY tested the January 30, 2004, high, it did

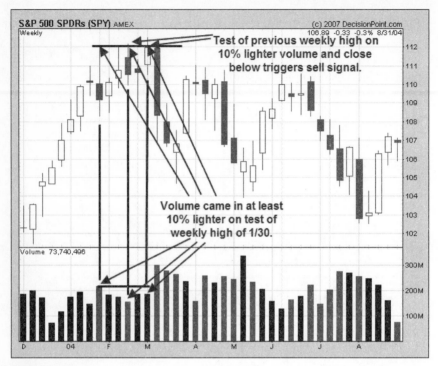

FIGURE 6.10   Volume Analysis of SPY Shows Volume Decline as January 30, 2004, High Is Tested in February and March
Source: Chart courtesy of DecisionPoint.com.

not have enough energy (volume) to get through that level. That high was rejected twice and triggered sell signals in the week of February 20 and March 5. The decline finally started the week of March 12.

Let's examine the Ord-Volume method for the same time frame for SPY. In Figure 6.11, look at the first down leg from the 116.5 level in late January 2004. Volume on this down leg came in at 56 million, which is a 75 percent increase in energy from the previous up leg that had volume of 32 million. This condition shows that downside energy is starting to take control and is a bearish sign.

The next up leg has volume of 33 million, which is a 41 percent decline in energy compared to the volume for the previous down leg of 56 million. This shows that the downward energy is still in control. For a rally phase to continue, the up leg should have more energy than the down leg, and in this case the opposite is occurring. SPY rallies to a new high at 116.97, but with no expansion in Ord-Volume, which comes in at 34 million and 23 percent less than the previous down leg. This effectively

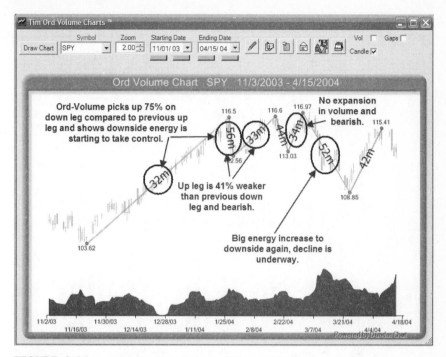

FIGURE 6.11   First Down Leg from 116.5 in SPY Shows a 75 Percent Increase in Volume Compared with Previous Up Leg—a Bearish Sign

kills the rally attempt. On the next leg down, Ord-Volume expands to 52 million, which has 53 percent more energy than the previous up leg. This big expansion in Ord-Volume shows a decline is under way.

Indexes do not have volume contractions and expansions that are as pronounced as what we see in equities. Therefore, we compare volume using bigger time frames to determine what the energy of the up leg and down leg energy is indicating, and to see if there is evidence that an index is nearing a high or low. The shift in energy from down to up or up to down can be seen easily seen in the Ord-Volume format for the current SPY example.

Let's look at what the NYSE McClellan Oscillator was saying for this same time frame. In Figure 6.12, we can see that the first step of the Summation Index sell signal setup occurred when the second high in the Summation Index was lower than the first high, while the NYSE was making a higher high. (I have labeled these events as "1" and "2" in Figure 6.12.) As explained earlier in the chapter, these conditions showed that fewer issues were carrying the market higher and a bearish breadth divergence existed.

FIGURE 6.12 McClellan Oscillator for NYSE Examines Corresponding Time Frame for Bearish Setup in SPY as Shown in Figure 6.11
Source: Chart courtesy of DecisionPoint.com.

The next step of the sell signal setup using the McClellan Oscillator was when the second low of the Summation Index traded below the first low, which showed downside momentum in advance/decline line. (I have labeled this event as "3" in Figure 6.10). The last step was when the Summation Index turned down again and a sell signal was triggered. These events came right at the high and help to confirm the sell signal using the volume methods explained in Figures 6.10 and 6.11.

MOMENTUM ANALYSIS

Now let's take a look at momentum indicators in this same time frame to see how this analysis also helps to identify tops. In Chapter 2, I gave a brief description of a momentum indicator, explaining that it smooths out price fluctuations of an issue so it is easier to see what direction price is moving. When a momentum indicator is rising, that issue is in an uptrend, and when the momentum indicator is declining, that issue is in a downtrend.

Using PMO, MACD Indicators

Of all the momentum indicators out there, I like PMO, developed by Carl Swenlin. This proprietary indicator is based on a rate-of-change calculation, which is exponentially smoothed. PMO behaves similar to the MACD momentum oscillator developed by Gerald Appel. We use the weekly PMO and MACD on the indexes to pick trends that usually last from three to six months.

Figure 6.13 shows the topping process in the S&P 500 in January to March 2004, as discussed previously. Notice here that both the PMO and MACD indicators had bearish crossovers and triggered sell signals in early March 2004, which predicted a decline that would last several months. The next bullish weekly crossover on the PMO and MACD did not come until mid-October 2004; therefore, the decline from the March high lasted seven months. During this time frame, traders would have been out of the market or short.

Also notice a bullish weekly crossover of PMO and MACD came in March 2003, and both PMO and MACD trended higher into March 2004, which would have kept traders long for an entire year. This was a good time to be in the market because traders clearly had the wind at their backs. Note that PMO gave a clearer view to stay long from March 2003 to March 2004 than MACD, which is one of the reasons I prefer PMO over MACD.

Next, let's examine the bullish crossovers of PMO and MACD in SPY, from early 2004 to early 2007, and compare them with the bullish signals generated by McClellan Summation Index in the same time frame. PMO and MACD buy signals are illustrated in Figure 6.14, and the bullish signals triggered by McClellan Summation Index are represented in Figure 6.15.

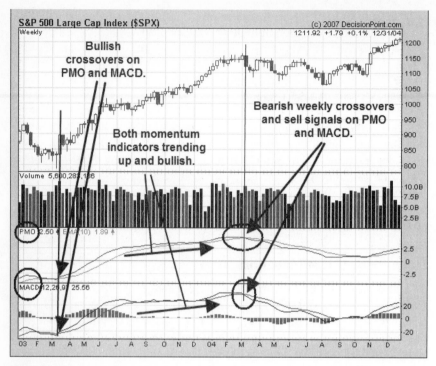

FIGURE 6.13   Momentum Indicators PMO and MACD, Highlighting Bearish Weekly Crossovers that Triggered Sell Signals in March 2004
Source: Chart courtesy of DecisionPoint.com.

Remember, a bullish signal is triggered when the Summation Index trades below −500 and then turns up.

In all instances the Summation Index triggered buy signals before PMO and MACD had bullish crossovers. Also notice that, in most cases, MACD had earlier buy signals than PMO.

To complete the buy signal setup, let's take a zero in on one of the bottoms and do a volume analysis of that low. Figure 6.16 focuses on the April 2005 bottom. A "Selling Climax Day" (see Chapter 4) occurred on April 15, 2005, with volume near 2.85 billion shares in the S&P 500. The next day, the price low was put in, which became the target for a future retest. On April 20, a "False Break" occurred with low volume that implied the decline would not continue.

A retest of that same low came on April 29 on lighter volume, which was another buy signal. Referring back to Figure 6.15, we can see that this bottom corresponded exactly with the Summation Index triggering a buy signal by turning up from below −500. Traders who had done

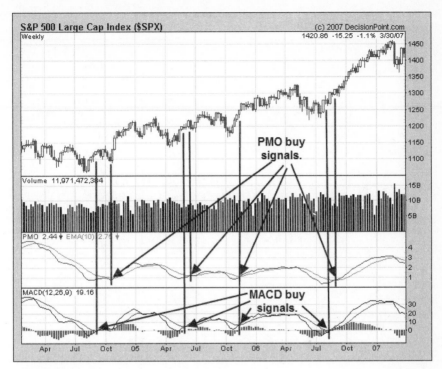

FIGURE 6.14 PMO and MACD Indicators Trigger Buy Signals in SPY during 2004–2007 Time Frame
Source: Chart courtesy of DecisionPoint.com.

these analyses would have known it was time to get long the market, and really would have put the wind at their backs. More conservative investors could have waited for the weekly PMO and/or MACD to turn up, or they could have bought and put stops below the price low of the "Selling Climax Day," just in case there were more retests of the recent lows. Having buy signals triggered by both breadth and volume analyses, however, the odds were very good that the momentum indicators would be turning up soon, as well.

Now let's switch to the bearish crossovers of the PMO and MACD in the time frame of early 2004 to early 2007, comparing them with the bearish signals generated by the McClellan Summation Index in that same time frame, as illustrated by Figures 6.17 and 6.18.

As Figure 6.17 shows, PMO and MAC sell signals are always after the top because price weakness needs to be present first in order for these indicators to turn downward. By contrast, the Summation Index (see Figure 6.18) measures breadth weakness as a top is approaching

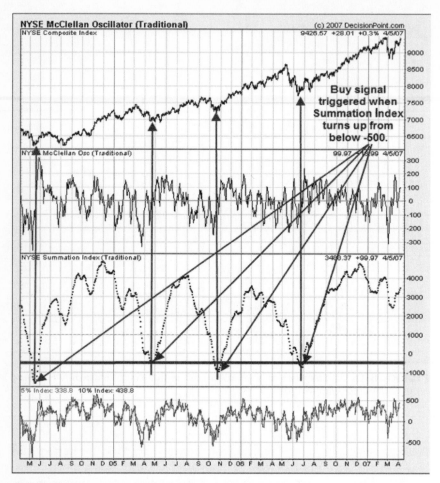

FIGURE 6.15   McClellan Oscillator Setups for Buy Signals in NYSE for 2004–2007, Corresponding to Figure 6.14
Source: Chart courtesy of DecisionPoint.com.

and give a "heads up" for potential topping patterns. Notice that the signals generated by both methods were very closely aligned time-wise in picking the same direction in the market. PMO and MACD did pick a top in early 2007, but the McClellan Summation Index negated that bearish signal by turning bullish (which occurred when the Summation Index traded above its previous high).

By combining breadth analysis with momentum analysis, traders can have more confidence when putting their money to work. (The volume

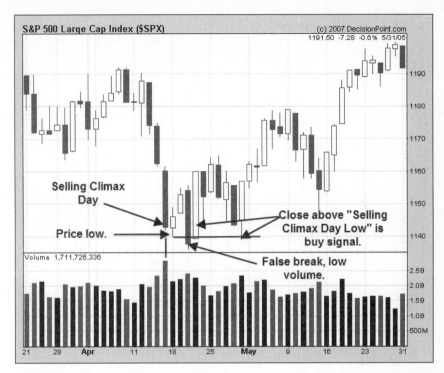

FIGURE 6.16 Snapshot of April 2005 Low, with Selling Climax Day Followed by False Break on Low Volume
Source: Chart courtesy of DecisionPoint.com.

analysis sell signal for SPY at the February and March 2004 high can be reviewed in Figures 6.10 and 6.11.)

Figures 6.19 and 6.20 spotlight the high in August and September 2005 in the SPY. Figure 6.19 is a weekly candlestick chart. The week of August 5 tested the previous high at 124.74 on lighter volume and closed below the previous week's high, which triggered a sell signal. The volume during the week of August 5 was not enough energy to get through the weekly high of July 28, and therefore the market reversed.

Notice that on the week of August 5, volume did not shrink a great deal, which is only a weak sell signal. As stated in Chapter 4, the greater the degree of volume shrinkage on a retest of a previous high, the stronger the sell signal. The weekly August 5 test of the previous high of July 29 had only a minor degree of shrinkage in volume, and therefore a weak sell signal resulted.

The market did go down for a month and then rallied back to test the weekly July 29 high during the week of September 9. Notice that the

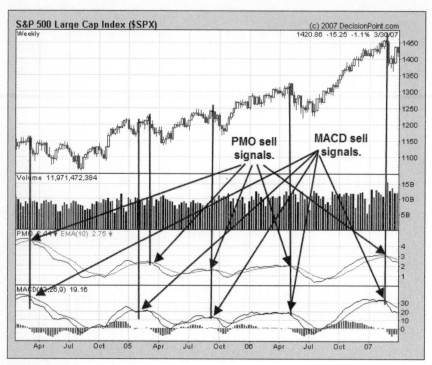

FIGURE 6.17   PMO and MACD Sell Signals Generated in SPY in the 2004–2007 Time Frame
Source: Chart courtesy of DecisionPoint.com.

weekly September 9 test of the July 29 high came on much reduced volume and triggered a stronger sell signal compared to the sell signal on August 5. The weekly sell signal of September 9 lines up well with the bearish crossover of the PMO momentum indicator and the McClellan Summation Index sell signal in September 2005, as shown in Figure 6.18. Therefore, the week of September 9 generated the better sell signal.

Figure 6.20 (on page 133) shows the Ord-Volume chart of SPY for the same time frame. Although it's not depicted here, Ord-Volume did generate a sell signal at the late July/early August high. However, Ord-Volume indicated much more going into the September 2005 high.

From the late August 2005 low, Ord-Volume had a strong first up leg of 83 million as the market hit a high of 123.15. This was followed by a weak down leg with Ord-Volume of 47 million, which implied that the uptrend should continue because there was more energy pushing upward than downward.

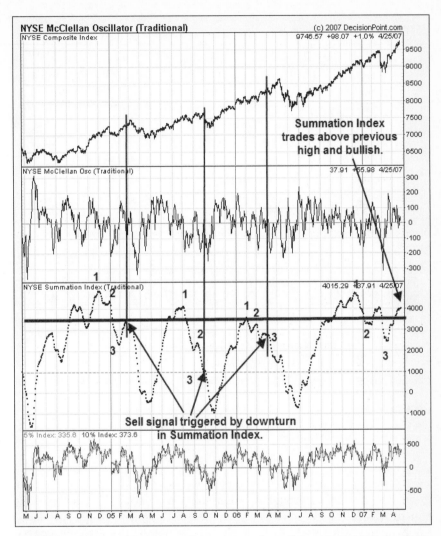

FIGURE 6.18 McClellan Oscillator Setups for Sell Signals in NYSE for 2004–2007, Corresponding to Figure 6.17
Source: Chart courtesy of DecisionPoint.com.

The next up leg tells a lot about the upward strength in the market. Ord-Volume on that up leg declined to 45 million—nearly half the energy of the previous up leg. This shows that the uptrend is very weak. Normally, indexes do not have this degree of volume shrinkage from one leg to another as stocks do. When an index does have volume shrinkage of this magnitude, it is showing that there is a great deal of weakness in that

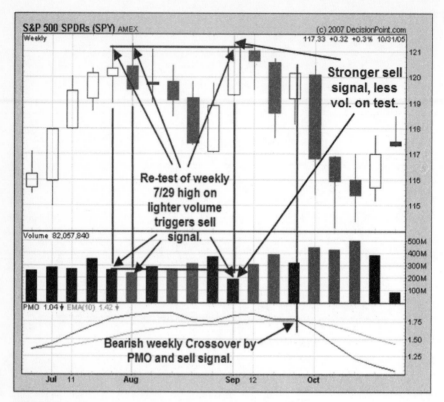

FIGURE 6.19   Candlestick Chart for SPY Shows a Retest of the Weekly July 29 High

Source: Chart courtesy of DecisionPoint.com.

trend. A sell signal was triggered when the SPY closed below the previous high of 123.15.

Notice on the down leg from the 124.74 high Ord-Volume increased by 50 percent to 68 million compared to the previous up leg volume of 45 million going into the 124.74 high. This increase in volume on the down leg confirmed the downtrend. (See Chapter 3 to review Ord-Volume techniques.)

Increasing Profits with the "Wind at Your Back"

As we've seen in this chapter, breadth analysis using the McClellan Summation Index, volume analysis using Ord-Volume and price and volume relationships, and momentum analysis with PMO and MACD indicators

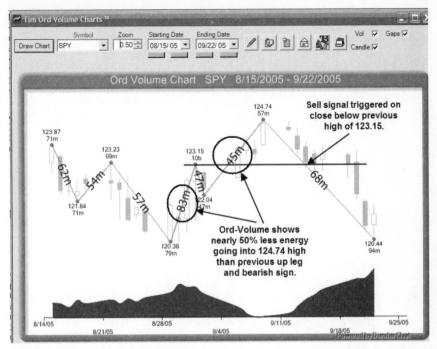

FIGURE 6.20   Ord-Volume Chart for SPY Focusing on the September 2005 High

all complement each other to help find the trends of the market. By finding the trend of the market first and then trading stocks in the direction of that trend, a trader is more likely to realize more winning trades. In effect, what a trader is attempting to do is trade from the long side when the advancing issues are increases and the declining issues are decreasing, and when volume is increasing on advancing issues and pushing them higher. This is the formula for success in the market.

In the next chapter we will focus on sector analysis to find the best stocks in strong sectors. We will also look at some indicators that I have found along the way that can confirm trends and reversals. And always remember, "Keep the wind at your back."

CHAPTER 7

Sector Analysis and Stock Analysis

The Importance of Sentiment

The goal of every trader is to make trades in which risk is the lowest and profit potential is the highest. The optimum opportunity to make such trades is when the market is at an extreme bottom and starting to rise.

To identify these trades, you must undertake breadth analysis, volume analysis, and momentum analysis, as discussed in Chapter 6, to identify bullish setups. These analyses must come first in order to have the "wind at your back"—the most favorable market conditions, which I have referred to several times. You cannot engage in sector analysis and stock analysis until you have determined that the overall market is in your favor (thus putting the wind at your back). Otherwise, the reliability of the signals generated by sectors and stocks will not be as accurate.

Once you know the market conditions are ripe for making a trade, you can buy virtually any stock and most likely it will be a profitable move because, as the saying goes, a rising tide raises all boats. Aphorisms aside, it is at these extreme lows when the market begins to move higher that you will find maximum profit potential. In order to reap the best potential results, you will need to identify which sectors and which stocks within these sectors will likely lead the way up on the rally phase. By identifying the best stocks within the strongest stock sectors to buy at extreme lows, you will maximize your profits as the market rallies upward.

While this probably sounds good, it raises the question: How do you find the strongest sectors at a market low? The answer lies in retracement relationships.

SECTOR AND STOCK ANALYSIS

Given what we've discussed thus far in the book, it makes sense that a strong sector will not go down as much during a market decline as a weak sector. A sector that retraces the least compared to other sectors during a market decline should be among the sectors that leads the next rally phase. Think about it: If a sector doesn't go down as much compared to other sectors during a market correction, then this is a stronger sector and should be a leader in the next market advance.

The overall market can be divided into more than 30 sectors, and some can be split further into additional sectors. To keep it simple here, we will use the nine sector sections used by John Murphy, a noted trader and market technical analyst. The nine sectors he thinks are the most important to track are: Banks Index ($BKX), Gold & Silver Index ($XAU), Semiconductor Index ($SOX), Oil Services ($OSX), Drug Index ($DRUG), Retail Index ($GSPMS), Internet Index ($DOT), Biotechnology ($BTK), and Broker-Dealers ($XBD).

In this chapter, we compare these nine sectors to each other from when the market was at a top to when it was at a bottom, in order to see which ones held up the best during market declines. The sectors that held up the best during the decline will be compared again on the next rally phase to show how this method of identification and selection would have performed.

Using Performance Comparisons to Find the Strongest Sectors

Figure 7.1 is a weekly chart of the S&P 500 ($SPX) going back to 2002. I have labeled the highs and lows on the chart as Top 1, Double Bottom 1, Double Top 2, Bottom 2, and so forth, in order to identify the decline and advance periods that we will be discussing.

As we begin, let's focus on the section of Figure 7.1 from "Top 1" to the low at "Double Bottom 1." Top 1 occurred in early March 2004, after which the market declined into a double bottom in May and again in August 2004, as labeled on the chart.

Turn your attention now to Figure 7.2, which is a line chart of the nine sectors in that time frame displayed together so that a trader can see the performances of each sector compared to the others. The sectors that stayed near the top of this chart performed the best from the March top to the decline at the May–August double bottom. These sectors would likely be the ones in which to buy stocks for the next rally phase.

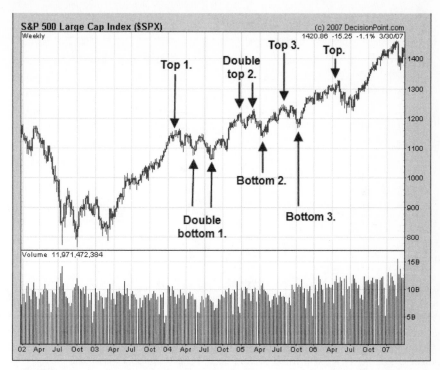

FIGURE 7.1   S&P 500 Chart Showing Highs and Lows Going Back to 2002
Source: Chart courtesy of DecisionPoint.com.

As Figure 7.2 shows, the best-performing sectors that went down the least from the March 2004 high to the May and August 2004 lows were the Internets Index and the Oil Services Index. Looking ahead on the time frame, at the top formed in December 2004, the Oil Services Index was up 30 percent and the Internet Index was up 33 percent, which was not a bad performance for a four- to seven-month time frame.

At this point, we know that at the double-bottom low in May–August 2004, the Internet Index and the Oil Services Index were the two sectors that had held up the best. Now, we want to find the strongest stocks within these two sectors. To pick the strongest stocks within a sector, you can apply the same performance comparisons that we have done with the sectors. The objective is to compare the performance of all stocks within a sector to see which ones held up the best (meaning they had the smallest percentage of retracement) going into the lows. Just as with the sectors, the thinking here is the stocks that retraced the least during a market decline should also lead the way up during an advance.

Major US Markets PerfChart

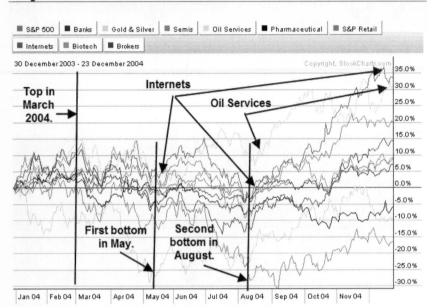

FIGURE 7.2   Line Chart that Shows All Nine Sectors, with Internets and Oil Services as the Best-Performing Sectors during the Targeted Time Frame
Source: Chart courtesy of StockCharts.com.

Comparing Stock Performances within a Strong Sector

Figure 7.3 is a line chart of the ten major stocks within the Internet sector: Amazon (AMZN), Aquantive (AQNT), Juniper Networks (JNPR), United Online (UNTD), Research in Motion (RIMM), Qwest Communication (Q), Priceline.com (PCLN), Qualcomm (QCOM), Monster Worldwide (MNST), and Earthlink (ELNK). The chart shows the performance of the stocks relative to each other.

The two Internet stocks that held up the best in this group going into the lows of the May and August double bottom were Research in Motion (RIMM) and Priceline.com (PCLN). RIMM tacked on about 110 percent from the May low and was the best performer of the group—and significantly outperformed the sector of the whole, which was up 33 percent. PCLN rallied about 20 percent from its August low, which was an underperformance compared with the sector overall.

A trader could also undertake a bigger study by selecting, say, 50 stocks and then comparing 10 at a time to find the best two of each group. The trader would take another 10 and select the best 2, and so forth, until

PerfChart
(AMZN,AQNT,JNPR,UNTD,RIMM,Q,PCLN,QCOM,MNST,ELNK)
Interactive Performance Comparison Chart

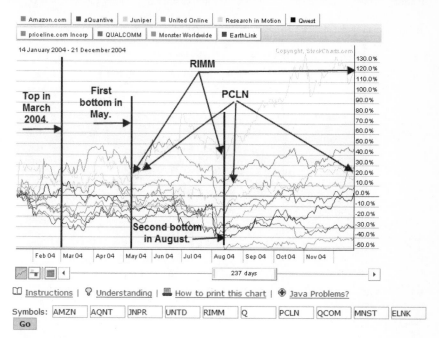

FIGURE 7.3   Line Chart that Shows the Performance of 10 Major Stocks within the Internet Sector
Source: Chart courtesy of StockCharts.com.

all 50 stocks were analyzed. The end result would be the 10 best stocks (the top 2 from each grouping), which would then be compared to each other. This would require more work, but the resulting performance should be better because a trader is looking at the strongest stocks within a group of 50 instead of only 10.

In Figure 7.4, we compare the performance of 10 of the major Oil Services stocks to each other, focusing on the time frame of the double bottom in May and August 2004. The 10 Oil Service stocks in this study were Global Industries (GLBL), Weatherford (WFT), National Oilwell Varco (NOV), Baker Hughes (BHI), Smith International (SII), Tidewater (TDW), Halliburton (HAL), Schlumberger (SLB), Cooper Cameron (CAM), and GlobalSantafe (GSF).

Looking at Figure 7.4, we can see that the two stocks that held up the best going into the lows were National Oilwell Varco (NOV) and

PerfChart
(GLBL,WFT,NOV,BHI,SII,TDW,HAL,SLB,CAM,GSF)
Interactive Performance Comparison Chart

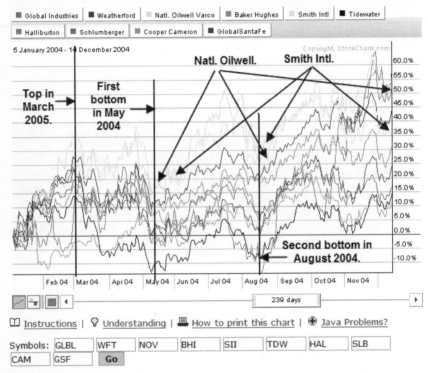

FIGURE 7.4   Line Chart Showing the Relative Performances of 10 Major Stocks in the Oil Services Sector
Source: Chart courtesy of StockCharts.com.

Smith International (SII). As the market rallied into December 2004, NOV advanced about 30 percent from its May low, while SII gained about 15 percent from its May low. These were the overall top in performers of those ten stocks in that rally phase. By comparison, the S&P 500 was up about 7 percent in this time frame.

The next high in the S&P 500 came in as a double top formed in January and March 2005 (which is labeled on Figure 7.1 as Double Top 2), followed by a pullback to a bottom in late April (Bottom 2), and then a rally to a high in August 2005 (Top 3).

Referring to Figure 7.5, the best performing sectors going into the April 2005 bottom were Brokers and Oil Services. At the April low

Major US Markets PerfChart

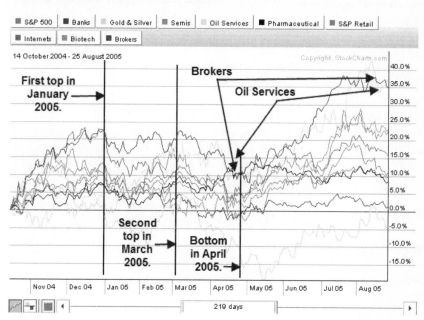

FIGURE 7.5   Comparison of Sector Performance, Focusing on the April 2005 Bottom to the August 2005 High
Source: Chart courtesy of StockCharts.com.

the Broker sector was up about 10 percent and tacked on another 25 percent to reach an overall gain of 35 percent as of the August high. The Oil Services sector was up about 15 percent at the April low and gained another 20 percent to also accumulate a 35 percent increase. The performance from the April low showed Brokers up 25 percent and Oil Services up 20 percent, compared to the S&P, which rose about 10 percent in this time frame.

Looking at the performance of the two sectors from the April low—Brokers, which rallied 25 percent, and Oil Services, which gained 20 percent—we can see that both posted double the performance of the S&P, which was up 10 percent in this time frame.

The next sequence would be to pick 10 (or more) stocks in the Brokers sector, comparing their performances to each other going into the April 2005 low. The two or three brokerage stocks that held up the best going into that low will be the candidates for purchase. The same analysis would then be done with the Oil Services stocks.

Stock Leadership Rotation   As of this point in time, the Oil Services stocks had been strong for a while, and a trader might expect a rotation in strength to different Oil Services stocks. Let's zero in on the April 2005 bottom and then look forward in time to see if leadership changed within the sector group, as displayed in Figure 7.6.

Figure 7.6 displays the same stocks as in Figure 7.4: Global Industries (GLBL), Weatherford (WFT), National Oilwell Varco (NOV), Baker Hughes (BHI), Smith International (SII), Tidewater (TDW), Halliburton (HAL), Schlumberger (SLB), Cooper Cameron (CAM), and GlobalSantaFe (GSF). As the chart shows, the Oil Services stocks that held up the best going into the April 2005 low were Baker Hughes (BHI) and Global Industries (GLBL). In the example of Figure 7.4, the strongest stocks in the Oil Services

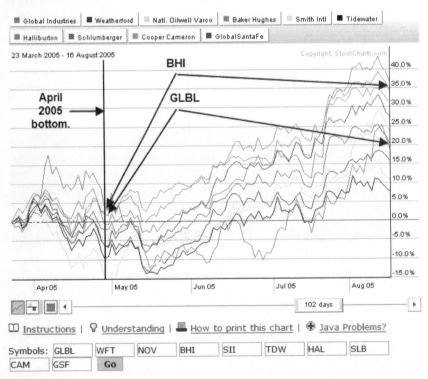

FIGURE 7.6   Comparison of Top Stocks within Oil Services Sector to Determine If Leadership in Sector Changed
Source: Chart courtesy of StockCharts.com.

sector were National Oilwell (NOV) and Smith International (SII). The point of repeating this study of the Oil Services stocks is to acknowledge that things change within a sector and new leadership develops. This leadership rotation can be recognized by doing a stock performance comparison study. The rewards of the extra effort involved can be an increase in the trading dollars you put into your pocket.

Examining Sectors in a Different Time Frame

The next time frame we examine is the top formed in August 2005 (labeled Top 3 on Figure 7.1) and the October 2005 bottom (labeled Bottom 3 on Figure 7.1). The next top came in February 2006. Looking at Figure 7.7, we can see that the two sectors that retraced the least going into the October 2005 low were Gold & Silver and Brokers.

At the October 2005 low, the Gold & Silver sector was up about 15 percent and continued to rally to an increase of 60 percent, for a net gain of 45 percentage points from the October low. Brokers were up about 10 percent at the October low and continued to rally to post a gain of 40 percent, for a net increase from the October low of 30 percentage points.

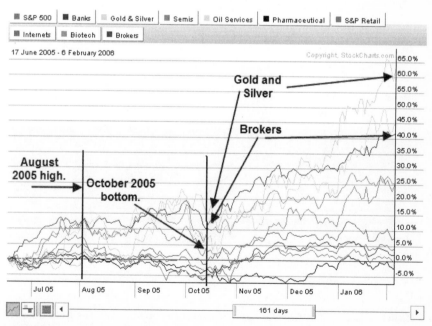

FIGURE 7.7   Comparison of Sector Performance from the August 2005 High to the October 2005 Low
Source: Chart courtesy of StockCharts.com.

By comparison, the S&P 500 was down about 3 percent at the October low, and then rallied to up 5 percent at the February 2006 high, for a net gain from the October low of about 8 percentage points. Therefore, the Gold & Silver and Brokers sectors outperformed the S&P 500 in this time frame by 400 percent or so. As this example clearly illustrates, by selecting the strongest sectors during a bull move, traders stand the best chance of being able to increase their returns significantly.

Focusing on Top Gold and Silver Stocks   Figure 7.8 shows a comparison of 10 top gold and silver stocks, which are Freeport McMoran (FCX), Harmony Gold Mining (HMY), Silver Standard Resources (SSRI),

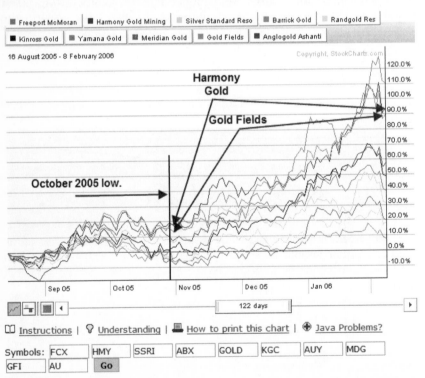

FIGURE 7.8   Chart Comparing Performances of Top Gold Stocks from October 2005 Low as the Market Rallied Higher
Source: Chart courtesy of StockCharts.com.

Barrick Gold (ABX), Randgold Resources (GOLD), Kinross Gold (KGC), Yamana Gold (AU), Meridan Gold (MDG), Gold Fields (GFI), and Anglo-Gold Ashanti (AU).

The two gold and silver stocks that held up the best going into the October 2005 low were Harmony Gold (HMY) and Gold Fields (GFI). Both issues were up about 20 percent at the October 2005 low and continued to rally into February 2006 to post increases of 90 percent, for a net gain of 70 percentage points for each. Again the S&P 500 in that time span saw an 8 percentage point gain in performance. Therefore, these gold issues outperformed the S&P 500 by nearly 900 percent.

A trader can pick the sectors and issues within those sectors that go down the least (or hold up the best) during a market decline, and assume that they will likely be the leaders on the next rally phase. The majority of the time, this will work just fine. For additional confirmation of bullish set-ups for sectors and issues in those sectors, refer back to Chapters 3, 4, and 5 to get specific buy and sell signals using price and volume relationships. This added confirmation and effort on your part should help increase your confidence and produce additional gains on the next rally phase in the market. The only reason a trader is in the market is to maximize profit. The methods and rules provided in this chapter and the previous six are meant to convey a methodology to help reach your financial goals.

INVESTOR SENTIMENT HELPS PICK MARKET TURNS

Another force that has a strong impact on market direction is investor sentiment. Investor sentiment should be used in conjunction with technical analysis to help complete the market direction picture. Investor sentiment is the public opinion on market direction. When public opinion is nearly balanced between the bulls and bears, then the general, prevailing trend at the time should continue—whether upward or downward. When public opinion becomes extreme, either bullish or bearish, then expect the trend to reverse against the public opinion.

The poet Robert Frost had it right when he wrote about taking the road less traveled. When it comes to market opinion, the road less traveled is the path a trader should take to capitalize on market direction. In the trader's quest to buy low and sell high, investor sentiment helps to identify market conditions that provide those types of opportunities.

Near tops in the market, the majority of investors are the most bull-ish, and at bottoms they are the most bearish. There are degrees in sentiment just as there are degrees of turns in the market, from minor to major.

For example, public opinion is usually stubbornly bullish at major tops. However, when public opinion switches easy from bullish to bearish, it is usually a more minor top. The reverse occurs at bottoms.

To help complete the flow of funds from "dumb money" (public market opinion) to "smart money" (trading the opposite of public market opinion), traders need to have at their disposal indicators that define in real money terms what the dumb money investors are doing. Notice I used the phrase *real money terms*, which means investors are putting real money at stake on their decisions, rather than just expressing what they think. Therefore, these decisions reflect actions instead of only opinions.

Dumb money can report being bearish on the market and relate that in an opinion poll such as "Market Vane Bullish Percent" or the "Consensus Bullish Sentiment Index of Market Opinion," while still being long in the market. However, when dumb money is short the market (taking positions in which profits are realized if the market goes down) in real money terms, then that carries more weight because it reflects what investors are thinking and also doing.

Interpreting "Dumb Money" Actions

Analyzing the dumb money's actions (what these investors are doing) will provide a fairly accurate investor sentiment reading of the market. There are all sorts of investor sentiment gauges out there, some shorter term and others longer term. There are several sentiment gauges that I like best and that line up well with the "wind at your back" method outlined in Chapter 6.

The first sentiment indicator I will review here is the "Rydex Cash Flow Ratio." Rydex is a mutual fund company that has both a bear and bull funds for the S&P 500 and the Nasdaq. It publishes the total dollar amount of assets in each fund on a daily basis. This makes it possible to analyze sentiment based upon what investors are actually doing with real money.

Prior to 2003 the Rydex funds had relatively small amounts of cash and were subject to extreme movement in either direction. Things have changed since then, and after 2003 Rydex has more than 40 funds with billions of dollars in assets. This provides a very stable platform from which to derive accurate sentiment readings. Since Rydex has both bullish and bearish funds, a trader can see which way the public is investing as cash flow is going from bullish funds to bearish funds or vice versa. Rather than measure someone's opinion about market direction, the Rydex Cash Flow Ratio presents information as to whether people are actually putting money where their mouths are.

Rydex's most popular funds are based on the S&P 500 and the Nasdaq 100. Rydex makes the asset levels of these funds available to the public each evening. This information allows traders to determine group sentiment on the market by observing where these investors are placing their money. Like all contrary indicators, when these investors become so optimistic that the assets flowing into the bullish funds soar higher, it is usually a good sign that the market is nearing a top and soon will see prices decline.

Reading the Rydex Cash Flow Ratio   Figure 7.9 displays the Rydex Cash Flow Ratio in a chart format (courtesy of Decisionpoint.com). Using this chart format, traders can compare current patterns with previous periods in time to make a determination of whether the current level is bullish, bearish, or neutral.

The upper half of Figure 7.9 shows the S&P 500, and the lower half is the Rydex Cash Flow Ratio. Carl Swenlin of DecisionPoint.com came up with a very useful calculation for the Rydex Cash Flow Ratio. He calculates and charts daily and cumulative net cash flows, which is the actual cash entering and leaving each Rydex fund. This is done by calculating the amount that total assets in a fund should have changed, based upon the percentage of change per share of net asset value (NAV), assuming that no cash was added to or taken out of the fund. We then subtract this amount from the actual amount of total assets in the fund, and the result is the daily net cash flow. He abbreviates this formula by:

$$\text{Bear CFL} + \text{MM/Bull CFL}$$

where CFL stands for cash flow level, and MM stands for money market.

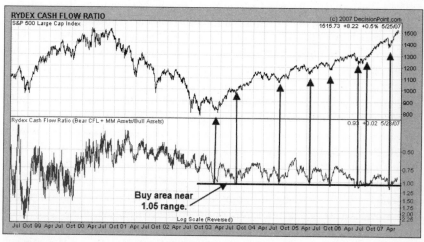

FIGURE 7.9   Rydex Cash Flow Ratio Chart Displays Ratio Readings at Lows in the S&P
Source: Chart courtesy of DecisionPoint.com.

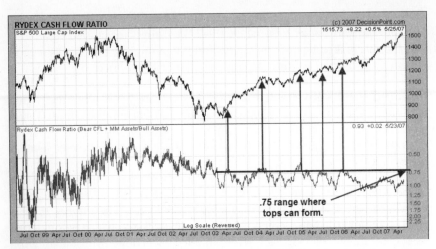

FIGURE 7.10   Rydex Cash Flow Ratio Chart Displays Ratio Readings at Highs in the S&P
Source: Chart courtesy of DecisionPoint.com.

This formula determines money flows in and out of the bullish and bearish Rydex Funds for the S&P 500 and gives an accurate sentiment view.

Referring to Figure 7.9, notice that since 2003, bottoms have formed in the S&P 500 when the Rydex Cash Flow Ratio reached near the 1.05 range. (Note the arrows pointing up from the 1.05 level). Readings in the 1.05 range suggests there is little interest on the long side for the S&P 500 among the public investor (dumb money), which is a bullish sign.

Figure 7.10 shows the Rydex Cash Flow Ratio where tops can form when this ratio reaches 0.75 or less. I have drawn arrows up to the S&P 500 to show this correlation with Rydex Cash Flow Ratio readings below 0.75. Notice that this particular sentiment gauge does not work as well for picking tops as it does for bottoms. However, we will turn to other sentiment tools that do work well in helping to pick tops in the market.

Put/Call Ratio–OEX Open Interest Ratio   Another sentiment indicator that is useful in picking turns in the market is the "Put/Call Ratio–OEX Open Interest Ratio." OEX is shorthand for the S&P 100 Index, which is made up of the 100 largest companies in the S&P 500. Open interest is defined as the total number of option contracts outstanding. The open interest ratio takes the total put open interest and divides it by the total call open interest. Therefore, a ratio of 1.80 indicates there are 1.8 put positions for every 1 call position.

The OEX put/call open interest ratio should be considered a noncontrarian sentiment indicator. Evidently, there are some very astute OEX option players out there who have got it right. Therefore, this sentiment indicator reflects the smart money. When this ratio becomes extreme expect a turn in the market.

Figure 7.11 shows that when the Put/Call Ratio–OEX Open Interest Ratio reaches 1.80 or higher, traders can expect the rally to end. At that point, either a sideways trading range or a market reversal would follow. The duration of time for this correction or consolidation phase should last a month or longer.

In Figure 7.12, when the Put/Call Ratio–OEX Open Interest Ratio reaches readings near 1.0 or lower, traders can expect a rally to begin shortly in the S&P 500. When the Put/Call Ratio–OEX Open Interest Ratio stays near 1.0 or lower for an extended period of time, the rally phase in the S&P 500 is expected to be extended.

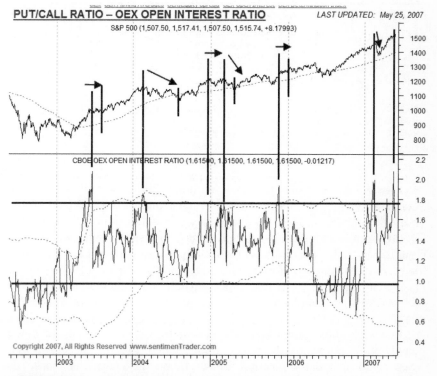

FIGURE 7.11 Put/Call Ratio—OEX Open Interest Ratio Readings at or Above 1.8 Indicate Market Highs
Source: Chart courtesy of www.SentimenTrader.com.

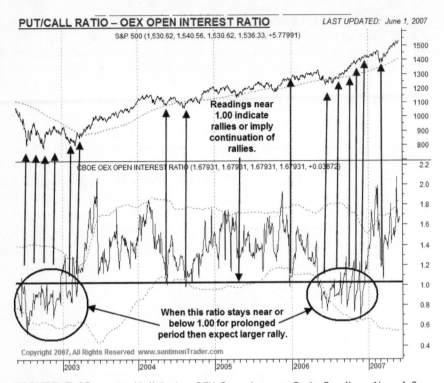

FIGURE 7.12 Put/Call Ratio—OEX Open Interest Ratio Readings Near 1.0 or Lower Indicate the Beginning of a Rally
Source: Chart courtesy of www.SentimenTrader.com.

Figure 7.13 illustrates the next sentiment indicator, "All-Index Small Speculator Positions." These statistics come from the Commodity Futures Trading Commission (CFTC), which is the regulatory body responsible for the futures industry. Essentially, this chart shows what small S&P commodity trader positions are. Normally, these players have the most long contracts, and therefore are the most bullish when the S&P 500 market is near a top, as we would expect. When positions held by the small S&P 500 speculators reach the 28 range, as Figure 7.13 shows, the S&P is near a top.

Likewise, these small S&P 500 speculators have a history of being heavily short at exactly the wrong time as well. Figure 7.14 shows that when small speculator positions reach 15 on the chart, the market is usually at a low.

Investor sentiment gauges help to find extreme highs and lows in the market for the shorter-term time frames, which lines up well with the

FIGURE 7.13 All-Index Small Speculator Positions Indicator Indicates When the Market Is Near a Top with a Reading Around 28
Source: Chart courtesy of www.SentimenTrader.com.

"wind at your back" method described in Chapter 6. To have confidence in a trading plan, traders need as much confirmation as possible of a top or bottom. By layering your technical analysis with investor sentiment gauges, you can become more confident of determining turns in the market to trade. If you don't do the necessary study to find market direction, you could find yourself in a precarious position—like standing on one foot at the edge of a cliff with a strong wind blowing. Any misbalance could hurt you.

Reading Short Interest for NYSE

Sentiment also can give a bigger view of the market. One sentiment gauge that provides a long-term view of the market is the short interest for the NYSE. First, understand that short selling allows a trader or speculator to profit when the market or a particular stock is declining. To short a stock,

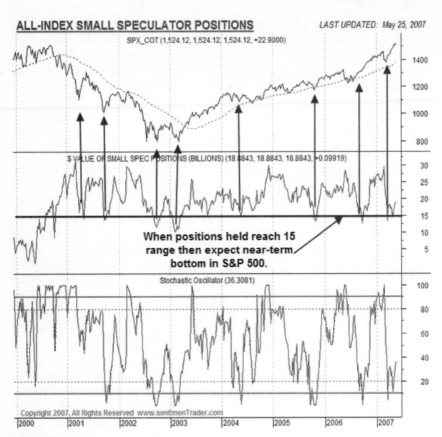

FIGURE 7.14   When All-Index Small Speculator Positions Indicator Is Around 15, the Market Is Likely Near a Bottom
Source: Chart courtesy of www.SentimenTrader.com.

a trader sells a security that he or she does not own. Rather, the short seller "borrows" a security and sells it, and then hopes to buy it back at a lower price later on, thus earning a profit when the borrowed security is returned. However, the security can also go up in price, and the trader must buy it back (covering the short position) at a higher price than what it was sold for, resulting in a loss.

Short interest reflects the total number of shares of a stock that have been sold short but not yet covered. The NYSE reports the total short interest for each stock once per month around the middle of the month. A large increase or decrease in short interest can be a good indicator of sentiment. A high short interest reading means that a large number of people believe that current prices are too high, and that the market or a particular security should decline. If a stock has relatively few shorts, then the majority of people believe that the market or a particular security should rally.

The short interest ratio is the total number of shares sold short (short interest) divided by average daily volume. Given an issue's average daily volume, it would take X number of days to cover the short position in that particular issue. The higher the ratio, the longer it would take to buy back the borrowed shares to cover a short position. That short covering, in addition to the normal buying of the issue, indicates just how bullish the issue potentially would become.

The exchanges also have short interest indicators that are simply the sum of all the individual short stocks traded at that exchange. The traditional way to calculate the short interest ratio of the NYSE is to take the short interest on all the stocks in that exchange and divide it by the average daily volume on the NYSE over the past month. A buildup of short interest is potentially bullish for the market because the shorts will eventually cover (providing buying power), which drives prices higher. Therefore, high short interest ratios tend to be bullish. Conversely, low short interest ratios mean that investors are basically bullish on the market. That, in turn, takes away the potential buying power of short covering, which tends to have a bearish effect.

Figure 7.15 shows the short interest ratio for the NYSE going back to 1990. The chart, provided by www.SentimentTrader.com, presents the data on a detrended basis, which is a means of looking at the data in such a way as to cancel out whatever long-term trend may be in place. In the case of short interest, increased hedging activity has skewed this indicator. The mathematical manipulation of volume and short interest (detrended) create an accurate presentation of what the chart is supposed to display.

Significant tops can occur when the Short Interest Ratio—NYSE (detrended) reaches near the −0.2 range, as happened at the 2000 top, represented by the largest arrow in Figure 7.15. Notice that from early 2006 to mid-2007, short interest increased from the −0.1 range to near 0.03, which at the time was a bullish, longer-term sign. This indicated that something similar may happen here as occurred from 1997 to 2000, when the market rallied significantly and squeezed off the shorts, taking the short interest ratio (detrended) ratio from 0.2 to −0.2.

As of this writing in mid-2007, the short interest ratio on the NYSE (detrended) gave a longer-term bullish signal and suggested the rally that started from the 2002 low still had much farther to go. Notice that the short interest ratio reading in mid-2007 was higher than the reading at the 2002 low. This condition suggested that because of the heavier short position in the market in mid-2007 compared to the 2002 bottom, the investing public was more bearish in mid-2007 than at the 2002 low.

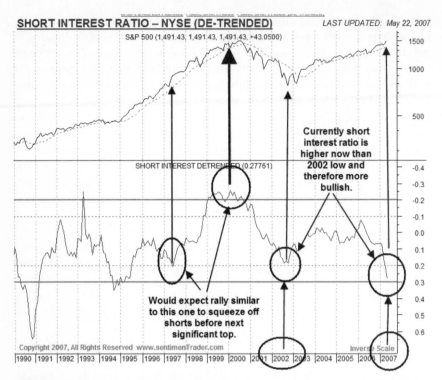

FIGURE 7.15   Short-Interest Ratio—NYSE Shows the Fluctuations in Short Interest as a Gauge of Bullish and Bearish Sentiment
Source: Chart courtesy of www.SentimenTrader.com.

When and if this ratio reaches the -0.2 range that will be the time a significant top may form.

Keep in mind that the Short Interest Ratio—NYSE (detrended) is only one indicator that was giving a longer-term bullish sign as of this writing. However, not all indicators work all the time, and it's fair to note that the short interest ratio could fail—just like any number of indicators that have failed in the past.

SUMMING IT UP: THE CONSENSUS OF INDICATORS

The key to successfully trading is to find as many indicators to confirm or deny the trend you are trading. When most of the indicators start to deny the trend, then it is time to pack up and leave that trend. There is not a "Holy Grail" indicator out there (at least I haven't found it) providing profitable trades every time. Rather, traders must use a consensus of indicators to light their way to financial trading success. In the previous chapters, I have outlined the indicators and methods that have worked for me, allowing me to achieve trading success. By taking time to study and review these chapters, traders should benefit from their efforts.

In the next chapter, we will look at how to put it all together, keeping it simple with a common-sense approach and covering the important topics of each chapter in sequential order. Your trading journey is nearly complete, and my hope is to give you a road map leading to your trading success.

CHAPTER 8

Gold Stocks

The Big Picture

M̲ost of the focus thus far has been on the broader equities market. Even when we focused on individual stocks, we began our study by determining the trend of the overall market first, and then worked our way through sectors, and finally focused on individual stocks. In this chapter, we are going to focus exclusively on one sector: gold.

Although it may not be associated as much these days with the "flight to quality" that accompanies war and global catastrophe, even the word *gold* evokes a feeling of security. Demand for gold is not just for investment purposes, but also for industrial and ornamental uses as well. All that aside, there is simply something about gold that captures an investors' attention—and maybe their imagination.

For me, I have focused on gold stocks since March 8, 2001, when my first purchase of a gold issue was Newmont Mining Corporation (NEM) at the price of $17.71. I became very interested in gold issues at this time because numerous technical indicators where pointing to the beginning of a very large bull market. Later in this chapter, I will cover what technical indicators were signaling a major move in the gold market back at the 2000 bottom. I will also explain what I see ahead for gold sector—including its next big target on the upside—and what indicators that may signal the next major top.

I'm proud to say that I was ranked the top gold timer of the year for 2005 according to *Timer Digest*, for the period from January 13, 2005, through January 13, 2006. I have consistently placed in the top five for the past three years for gold. I was also featured on the cover of the March 14, 2005, issue of *Timer Digest*.

I trade gold investments when I see that a major bull market is in process according to my technical analysis of the sector, and I know that this is where profits are likely to be accumulated. However, I do not speculate in gold by buying coins or bullion in order to own the physical commodity. I do so by trading the Gold & Silver Sector (XAU), which is listed on the Philadelphia Stock Exchange.

The Gold & Silver Sector (XAU) is a capitalization-weighted index comprised of 16 gold and silver mining industry stocks. Although I also trade individual gold stocks (as seen in earlier examples in the book), taking a position in XAU provides me with broader exposure to the sector in order to take advantage of both fundamental and technical factors that are influencing precious metals.

The stocks currently in XAU are: Agnico Eagle Mines Ltd. (AEM), Anglogold Ashanti Ltd. (AU), Barrick Gold Ltd. (ABX), Freeport-McMoran Copper & Gold Inc. (FCX), Gold Fields Ltd. (GFI), Goldcorp Inc. (GG), Harmony Gold Mining Company Ltd. (HMY), Kinross Gold Corporation (KGC), Meridian Gold Inc. (MDG), Newmont Mining Corporation (NEM), and Pan American Silver Corporation (PAAS). These gold stocks are considered the upper tier, and when combined into the XAU give a good representation of performance for the gold stock sector.

READING THE PRICE RELATIVE TO GOLD RATIO (PRTG)

In order to understand this sector, let's start with the big picture. Figure 8.1 is a weekly chart of XAU dating back to 1984. The upper window in the chart shows value of the XAU index. The lower window is the Price Relative to Gold Ratio (PRTG), which measures the discount or premium that XAU carries versus the price of gold as a commodity.

As Figure 8.1 shows, when the PRTG is at a low level, then the gold stocks comprising the XAU are cheap relative to the price of gold. Conversely, when the ratio is high, then the gold stocks in the XAU are selling at a premium compared to the price of gold.

This ratio is useful in determining whether gold stocks are cheap or expensive relative to gold prices, which helps to determine whether the XAU is near a high or low. The PRTG also gives investors a gauge of when to buy gold stocks at lows (when they are priced cheaply) and when to sell when at highs (when they are considered expensive).

Buy Signals Using the PRTG

Going back to 1984, major buy signals were triggered when the PRTG traded at 0.20 or below. Major buy signals (which are marked on Figure 8.1)

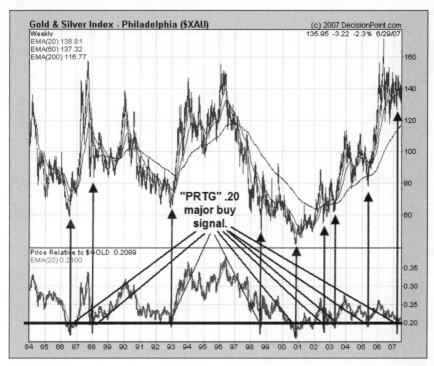

FIGURE 8.1   Buy Signals in Gold & Silver (XAU) Index Indicated by PRTG Falling to 0.20
Source: Chart courtesy of DecisionPoint.com.

were triggered on each major consolidation from the 2000 low. Specifically, the major consolidation lows of 2003 and 2005 coincide with a bullish PRTG reading of below 0.20. After PRTG registered below 0.20, major impulse rallies began in the XAU, which then rallied 67 percent and 112 percent after the lows in 2003 and 2005, respectively.

The last bullish signal came in March 2007 when the PRTG went below 0.20 on the daily chart near the 130 range. Once again, this was signaling that the gold stocks in the XAU were cheap and considered a buy based on their value relative to the price of gold.

Sell Signals Triggered by PRTG

Now that we've examined buy signals using the PRTG, let's look at the opposite scenario. Figure 8.2 shows what happens when the PRTG reaches above 0.33 and what that means for the XAU. Going back to 1984, we can see that major sell signals were triggered when PRTG traded above 0.33, which implied that the gold stocks comprising the XAU were expensive.

FIGURE 8.2 Sell Signals in Gold & Silver (XAU) Index Triggered When PRTG Hits Above 0.33
Source: Chart courtesy of DecisionPoint.com.

As Figure 8.2 illustrates, major sell signals were triggered in 1984, 1988, 1990, 1994, and 1996 by readings on the PRTG. Interestingly, notice that since the 2000 low in the XAU the PRTG has not reached the 0.33 range, which would have indicated that gold stocks were expensive and therefore generated a bearish signal.

I interpret this as a bullish sign for the XAU, meaning that gold stocks have not become expensive and overly "exuberant." Therefore, in general, I expect the XAU to work higher until the PRTG reaches the 0.32 level or higher. When PRTG reaches 0.32 or higher, then it will be time for traders to sell their gold stock holdings.

ELLIOTT WAVE ANALYSIS IN GOLD

As a disclaimer, I should state up front that I'm not an Elliott Wave expert. (To define briefly, Elliott Wave Theory is named after Ralph Nelson Elliott who believed that market movements could be predicted through repeating patterns of waves.) However, I do have some knowledge of these wave patterns (and a little knowledge can be dangerous!), and I have seen how well Elliott Wave Theory can be used to confirm other bullish indicators in regard to the XAU.

In Figure 8.3, I have labeled on the XAU chart what I believe to be the correct wave count from the 2000 low. As you can see, Wave 1 and Wave 3 in the XAU were about equal in length.

According to Elliott Wave Theory, there is usually one impulse wave that is extended, and most of the time that is either Wave 3 or Wave 5. Wave 3 was not extended (and neither was Wave 1), which implies that when Wave 5 occurs, it will be extended. If Wave 5 is extended, then it should be at equal in length to Waves 1 and 3 combined, which amounts to 120 points.

Looking at the chart, we can see that the Wave 4 low in October 2006 was near the 120 range on the XAU. Adding 120 points to the bottom of Wave 4, we can project that Wave 5 would have an upside target to the 240 range.

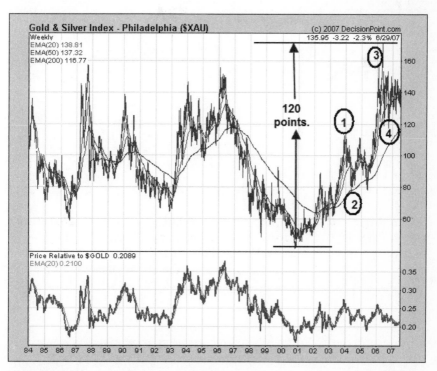

FIGURE 8.3 Elliott Wave Theory Applied to XAU
Source: Chart courtesy of DecisionPoint.com.

This type of projection adds to the already bullish outlook for gold. As stated earlier, the PRTG has not been in the 0.33 range, which would signal that gold stocks in the XAU are expensive compared to the price of gold. Further, Elliott Wave Theory points to the strong possibility of an extended wave in the future, which would take XAU up significantly.

USING "THIRD TIME UP" AND VOLUME ANALYSIS

As we study Figure 8.4, we can see that XAU has tested the 160 range three times: in 1987, 1996, and in 2006. The recent test of the 160 range for the third time produced a trading pattern known as "Third Time Up."

The Third Time Up pattern implies that the market will rally through that previous resistance. In addition, testing previous highs on higher volume also indicates that the previous high level will be exceeded. Although

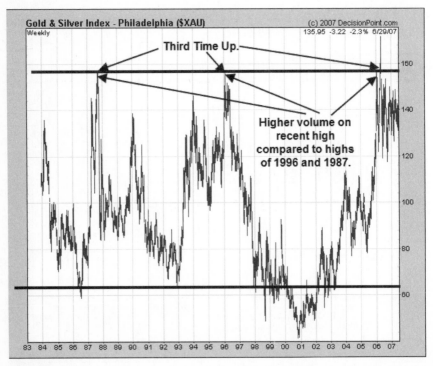

FIGURE 8.4   "Third Time Up" Trading Pattern Formed as XAU Tested 160 Range in 2006
Source: Chart courtesy of DecisionPoint.com.

I do not have the exact volume figures, I have estimated that the recent test of the 160 range was with nearly *10 times* the volume that occurred at the 1996 and 1987 highs. This volume analysis also strongly suggests that the 160 range will be exceeded.

APPLYING BREAKOUT ANALYSIS

Turning our attention to Figure 8.5, we can see what has happened in the past when XAU broke significant lows. In particular, we focus on the points between 1998 and 2002 (as indicated on the chart) when the XAU broke below the lows of 1986 and 1992 near the 62 range.

As the chart shows, the XAU was unable to hold the lows below 62 and closed above that level in 2002. This triggered another trading pattern called a "Shakeout," which is a failed breakdown to the downside that puts the market in a bullish condition. As traders know, if a market can't

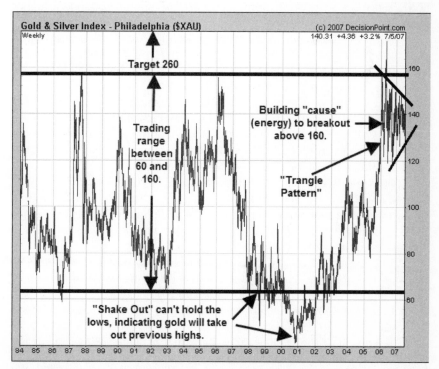

FIGURE 8.5   Breakout Analysis in XAU Shows Increased "Energy" to the Upside
Source: Chart courtesy of DecisionPoint.com.

hold below the previous low, then it will likely reverse and take out the previous highs.

What that means for the XAU could be significant. The XAU could very well take out the highs of 1987 and 1996 at the 160 range. Therefore, a very bullish signal was triggered in 2002 by the inability of the XAU to hold below the previous lows back in 1992 and 1986.

The current pattern in the XAU that started in May 2006 and is ongoing (as of this writing in July 2007) appears to be a "triangle" formation. Triangle patterns form at the mid of impulse waves and usually mark the halfway point of the next move higher. In "Richard Wyckoff terms," the consolidation triangle pattern is called "cause."

Cause shows the building of energy for the next move or impulse wave. Sideways pattern are necessary to build strength for the next impulse wave to follow. The longer the cause, the longer the time span for the next rally. Therefore, if a trader had a choice between two stocks, and one had been consolidating for one month and the other stock had been consolidating for three months, then the better choice would be the three-month consolidating stock. That longer consolidation stock would be poised for a longer-term rally and therefore should produce a higher percentage gain.

As of July 2007, the XAU had been building cause for more than a year, which should produce a rally phase that could also last a year or even longer. Notice in Figure 8.5 that the XAU is also building cause right below the breakout area near the 160 range.

When stocks or indexes consolidate, "hugging" near the breakout area, it is building energy to jump through the resistance zone. In the case with the XAU, it implies that energy is accumulating to jump over the 160 resistance range. In Richard Wyckoff terms, this type of rally through the highs would be "Jumping the Creek." (See Chapter 4.)

It is worth noting that a bearish sign would have developed if the XAU backed away from the 160 level and, say, traveled back to the 100 range as that would have met the criteria for a "Price Rejection." However, since the XAU is hugging the 160-range, it implies an eventual break through the 160 level and therefore is bullish.

Another method to find price projections for a stock or index is to measure the distance from the bottom of the trading range to the top of the trading range, and then add it to the breakout area. Since our current formation on the XAU is bullish, we will add this number to the 160 breakout level.

The bottom of the trading range back in 1992 and 1986 was near the 60 range, and the top of the trading range came at the highs of 1996 and 1987 near the 160 range. The difference is 100 XAU points. Now, adding

100 points to the breakout area at the 160 level gives an upside target at the 260 range.

As you recall from the Elliott Wave discussion earlier in this chapter, that analysis produced an upside target in the 240-range, which is fairly close to the result of this method. Clearly, then, we can see that the bigger picture for gold stock is bullish.

WHAT LIES AHEAD FOR GOLD

As I've laid out in this chapter, the longer term scenario for gold—looking at the sector using a variety of tools and analyses—is bullish. So what does that mean? Making predictions is not without risk, but let's take a look at what the analyses are telling us.

As of this writing, it appears that the recent low on the XAU may have already been seen at the October 2006 low near the 120 range. Further, the Price Relative to Gold (PRTG) reached the bullish 0.20 range in March 2007. The Elliott Wave count looks to be bullish, with the possibility of a Wave 5 extension. In addition, the "Third Time Up" trading method and the volume analysis for gold also point to a breakthrough to the upside.

The current consolidation is "hugging" the breakout area near the 160 range and suggest that a move to the upside is not far off. Therefore, my projection for the XAU is near 250.

When the 250 range on the XAU is achieved, if the PRTG hits or exceeds 0.32, then that would imply that the gold rally has reached its highs and gold stocks would be considered expensive. If these indications surface, then it would be time to sell.

CONCLUDING THE GOLD DISCUSSION

Although we used some different tools and methodologies to analyze the gold sector (XAU) there are some commonalities to the approach we applied in earlier chapters to indexes and stocks. For one thing, we looked at the bigger picture which, as I've stated before, always dominates the short term. Further, we studied at price action at significant highs and lows to observe what the market was telling us. Also, we analyzed volume and, looking at "cause," we determined the energy that was building up in the market.

Beyond the specifics of the gold market, perhaps the biggest lesson to take away is the fact that I did not base my premise or prediction on one indicator alone. We looked at several in order to build a consensus of opinion. As of this writing, the consensus of those indicators is a bullish sentiment for gold in the longer term.

As future scenarios play out in gold, I will continue to watch the indicators for signs of confirmation as the market moves higher, or for any surprise developments that change the market dynamics. My eyes always will be on the gold market and my attention focused on several different indicators to determine what this sector is telling me.

CHAPTER 9

Putting it All Together

Throughout this book, we have closely examined the elements of what I call the top-down approach to trading. We start at the top, determining the trend of the overall market in order to trade in alignment with it for a better potential outcome. Then we move down a step to identify the strongest sectors within the current market conditions (the theory being the sectors that have held up the best, or that have declined the least, during a market downturn, will likely lead the way in the next upturn). Once we have identified the strongest sectors, we look for the best stocks within those sectors using the same concept: focusing on those that have done the best in poor market conditions with the belief that they will probably post the strongest (or at least a strong) performance when the market rallies from a significant low or bottom.

We have also looked a variety of methods and techniques for identifying trade setups, concentrating on the *volume* within a specific index or issue. Rather than focus on price action, which can actually distract a trader, we look at percent changes in volume for what it tells us about the "energy" or force behind a particular upward or downward move. Using these tools we are able to "listen" to what the market is telling us and move in concert with it, rather than making random trades based on one signal or, worse yet, a hunch or something we've heard.

Now, in this chapter, we are going to put it all together. We're going to replicate the sequence of steps traders should take to create a successful game plan for winning in the market. As we begin, let's pretend for the moment that you have just returned from an extended period of travel, and you have not kept up with the movements of the market. You are coming back to the market blind; you don't know the levels of the New York Stock Exchange (NYSE), S&P 500, and Nasdaq or where they have been. Oh, and while we're at it, let's say it is 2002.

The best way to reacquaint yourself with the market is to check the sentiment reading. Although we addressed sentiment towards the end of this book (Chapter 7), I want to start there because sentiment readings provide you with a fairly accurate representation of where the market may be heading, and also give you some clues as to whether a high or low in the market may be near.

Throughout this book, I have talked about having the "wind at your back," which means that you want to have market dynamics in your favor before you make a trade. Therefore, before you start looking for the strongest sectors in the market and the best-performing stocks within those sectors, you will want to know whether the overall tone of the market is bullish or bearish. If it's bullish and you're looking to go long, then you'll have the wind at your back and enjoy a better chance of sailing along nicely. If the market tone is bearish and you're going long (or vice versa, the tone is bullish and you're looking to make a short trade), then the wind will be in your face—and could be blowing some dirt in your eyes as well.

After determining if the wind is at your back, I explained in previous chapters how to evaluate buy and sell signals on stocks using the Ord-Volume, Swing Price, and Volume Relationships methods. Before all of that occurs, however, traders need to gauge the sentiment of the market to determine if the trend is bullish or bearish, and whether a possible high or low is nearby.

STEP 1: READING MARKET SENTIMENT

The first step in determining market direction on the bigger time frame is to read the longer-term sentiment using the short interest ratio of the NYSE (detrended). We covered how to interpret short interest ratio (detrended), which is a reflection of the investor herd mentality or "dumb money," in Chapter 7 (see Figure 7.15).

Now, turning our attention to Figure 9.1, let's consider the scenario as presented in the opening of this chapter: You've been absent from the market for a while and you need to get back into the swing of things, starting with the current sentiment.

Studying the "Dumb Money"

When fear is running high among the dumb money, the Short Interest Ratio—NYSE (detrended) will be near or exceeding 0.2. As Figure 9.1

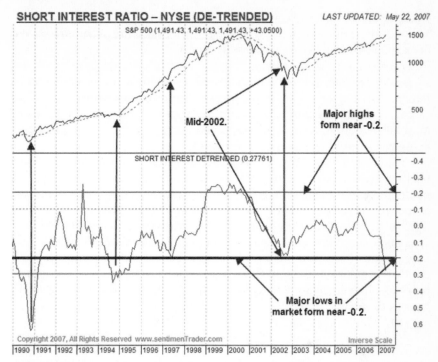

FIGURE 9.1 Short Interest Ratio—NYSE (Detrended) Chart Showing Correlation with Major Market Lows
Source: Chart courtesy of SentimenTrader.com.

shows, a reading at that level indicates that the market may be near a major low. Conversely, when the dumb money is showing signs of extreme confidence, then this ratio will be near -0.2 and possibly near a major high in the market.

Every trader knows that a major low in the markets was made in 2002. Returning from your sabbatical in mid-2002, however, you don't have that knowledge as yet. What you notice at this point is that the Short Interest Ratio—NYSE (detrended) was near 0.2, which is an area where major lows have occurred. This implies that the NYSE is nearing a major low. Therefore, instead of fearing that the market may continue lower, your confidence for a major bottom in the market is increasing.

The next sentiment indicator is useful in a shorter-term time frame; that is, the Rydex Cash Flow Ratio. As I explained in Chapter 7, Rydex is a mutual fund company that has both bullish and bearish funds for the S&P 500 and Nasdaq Composite. It publishes the total dollar amount of assets in each fund on a daily basis, which makes it possible to analyze sentiment based upon investors' cash flow into and out of the bullish and bearish funds. Therefore, we will be able to identify extreme sentiment among the dumb money investors on a shorter-term timeframe using the Rydex Cash Flow Ratio.

In Figure 9.2, the S&P 500 is in the top half of the graph, and the Rydex Cash Flow Ratio is on the bottom. Prior to 2003, Rydex funds had relatively small amounts of cash and were subject to extreme movement in either direction. Nonetheless, this ratio still gave a good indication of oversold levels when the ratio neared 0.75.

The Rydex Cash Flow Ratio shows that the dumb money flow into bearish funds in mid- to late 2002 was at an extreme compared to the money flow into bullish funds. This is another indication that the market was about to reverse to the upside. Looking ahead, notice that in early 2003 the Rydex Cash Flow Ratio hit a new three-year oversold level near 1.05, and in our view was a capitulation in that there was an extreme cash flow move to bearish fund. This was a very bullish sentiment reading and implied a major move up in the market was about to begin. Since 2003, this level in the Rydex Cash Flow Ratio has marked intermediate-term lows in the market.

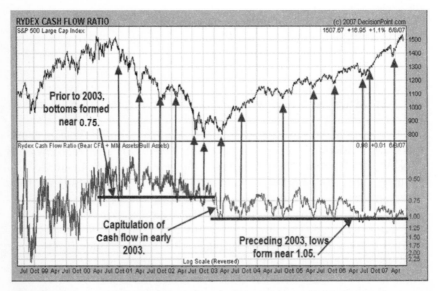

FIGURE 9.2   S&P Market Action Compared with Rydex Cash Flow Ratio
Source: Chart courtesy of DecisionPoint.com.

Now let's review for a moment: We know that, as of mid-2002, Short Interest Ratio—NYSE (detrended), which encompasses a longer-term view of the market, reached a bullish level. By early 2003 the Rydex Cash Flow Ratio (which provides an intermediate-term view of the market) hit capitulation, which sentiment-wise predicted a significant bottom. Therefore, between mid-2002 and early 2003, the sentiment on the larger time frame and intermediate-term time frame were very bullish.

There is another indicator that I would like to present, which is not a sentiment gauge per se, but it does reveal some interesting insights regarding whether the market is "sold out." Looking at Figure 9.3, we can see the percentage of NYSE stocks that were above their 200-day, 50-day and 20-day exponential moving averages (EMAs). This percentage helps to pick out major lows in the market that can sometimes last for years. This indicator does not need to be checked every day, but it is helpful to know where the percentage is at any given time.

We know that when a stock is above its 200-day, 50-day or 20-day EMA, it is trending upward and considered bullish for those time frames. A good way to determine if overall market conditions are overbought or oversold across a range of time frames is to analyze the percentage of stocks that are above their 200-, 50-, and 200-day EMA. We like to monitor the 200-day EMA to pick out significant lows in the market.

In Figure 9.3, the top window displays the NYSE going back to 1987 and the window below is a chart of the stocks in the NYSE that are above their 200-day EMA. During periods of time when only 20 percent of stocks are above their 200-day EMA, the market is oversold, based on bigger time frames, and near a major low. This indicator has helped pick out all the significant lows going back to 1987, and is a good gauge to keep in your bag of technical tools.

Notice that we have started with the longer-term indicators, working down to the shorter-term ones. This is because the longer-term rules over the shorter-term. Therefore, once we have identified the longer-term trend, we align our short-term indicators to that trend. That way we have "stacked the cards" in our favor and have increased our chances for success in the market. We are effectively pursuing the adage of "buying low and selling high."

Thus far, we have determined that sentiment on the longer-term and intermediate-term time frames were bullish and we suspect that—this being mid- to late 2002 in our scenario—a low was being put in. And the percentage of NYSE stocks above their 200-day EMA at an oversold level of below 20 percent, which is also bullish.

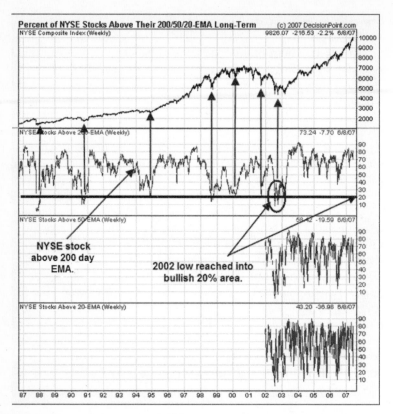

FIGURE 9.3 Charts Showing Percentage of NYSE Stocks above Their 200-, 50-, and 20-Day Exponential Moving Averages
Source: Chart courtesy of DecisionPoint.com.

STEP 2: EVALUATING BREADTH, VOLUME, AND MOMENTUM

The next step begins the top-down approach to the market by evaluating breadth, volume, and momentum. By evaluating these three factors our goal is to identify a trigger to enter the market.

Breadth—Using the McClellan Oscillator and Summation Index

We start the process with breadth. The tools we use are the McClellan Oscillator for the NYSE first, and then the McClellan Summation Index. In Figure 9.4, the NYSE is in the top window. The second window down

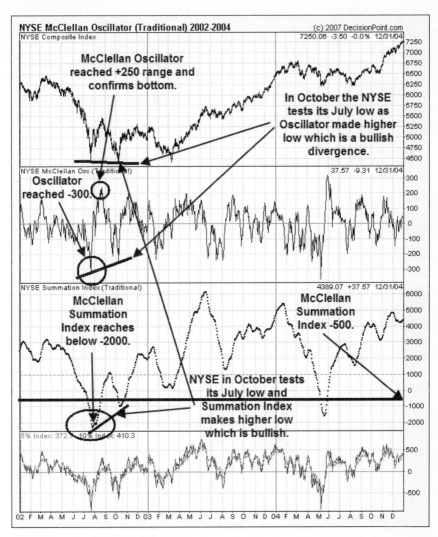

FIGURE 9.4 NYSE Displayed with McClellan Oscillator and McClellan Summation Index
Source: Chart courtesy of DecisionPoint.com.

is the McClellan Oscillator and third window down is the McClellan Summation Index.

In Chapter 6, I noted that readings below -230 on the McClellan Oscillator predict the market is at extreme oversold levels, which is the type of condition that appears near intermediate-term bottoms. Looking at

Figure 9.4, we can see that in July 2002, the McClellan Oscillator reached −300, which exceeded the requirement for a bottom. Therefore, this indicator is bullish for the short term.

In Chapter 6, I also wrote that once the McClellan Oscillator goes below −230 indicating indicate the NYSE has hit capitulation, to confirm a bottom in the NYSE the McClellan Oscillator should switch immediately and rally to +175 or higher to show that the advance/decline line has switched from down to up. In Figure 9.4, notice that the McClellan Oscillator reached the +250 range, which confirmed a bottom was made in the NYSE using the McClellan Oscillator method.

Also note in Figure 9.4 that after the McClellan Oscillator reached +250, a pullback started on the NYSE that took it down in October 2002, testing the levels of the July low in October. Then see that the Oscillator made a much higher low near the −200 range, which shows that the advance/decline line was getting stronger and a bullish divergence was emerging.

Moving on to the McClellan Summation Index method, recall that in Chapter 6, I stated that to pick a bottom in the NYSE, the first condition is that the Summation Index must be at an extremely oversold level of −500 or lower to indicate capitulation in the market. Referring back to Figure 6.9, see how no signal was generated until the Summation Index turns up from below −500. Once the Summation Index turned back up from below −500, this showed that the advance/decline line was now improving, and more issues were starting to carry the rally. This indicated a bullish condition.

Figure 9.4 shows how the McClellan Summation Index traveled all the way down below −2,000 in late July 2002, which implied a major oversold condition. The −2,000 reading on the McClellan Summation Index goes hand-in-hand with the extreme oversold reading in the percentage of NYSE stocks above their 200-day, 50-day, and 20-day EMA, as shown in Figure 9.3.

In this time frame, given what these indicators were saying, you would start to realize that something major may be developing in the NYSE. The McClellan Summation Index had turned up from below −2,000 in early August 2002 and triggered a buy signal by this method. Also notice in Figure 9.4 that the NYSE tested its July low in October, and the Summation Index made a much higher low and a bullish divergence was present. Therefore, the McClellan Oscillator and Summation Index produced bullish intermediate term signals.

Volume—Gauging the "Energy" of the Market

After determining the breadth of the market, the next evaluation step is volume analysis. In previous chapters, I stressed that volume is the force behind the movement of stocks and indexes. Volume pushes the indexes and stocks up or down, and the market goes in the direction of the legs with the highest volume. Tops (or bottoms) form in markets because energy to the upside (or downside) has run out. Volume is energy; therefore, when a market hits new highs (or lows) and volume shrinks, then the rally (or decline) is doomed to fail.

To do volume comparisons we look at previous weekly highs (lows) in the market and compare volume as those highs (lows) are being tested. On the test, we look to see if volume is equal to or greater than the volume of the previous high (low) to determine if the rally has sufficient energy to pass through the highs (lows), or if volume is at least 10 percent less, which means the highs (lows) will be rejected. This can be seen more clearly using longer time frames and weekly charts.

Figure 9.5 shows a weekly chart of the NYSE from January 2002 to December 2003. In mid-July 2002 the weekly volume expanded to a very high level of 12 billion shares and implied a possible "selling climax" may

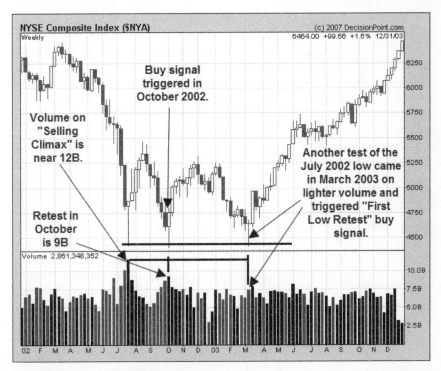

FIGURE 9.5 NYSE Weekly Chart, Focusing on Volume Comparisons at Selling Climax, Followed by Retest in October 2002
Source: Chart courtesy of DecisionPoint.com.

have occurred. The NYSE bounced for several weeks and came back down and tested the July 2002 low in October on volume of 9 billion shares and closed above the July low.

For a bullish signal to be triggered using the volume method, the NYSE needed to break the July 2002 low (which the NYSE did in October 2002). Further, the break had to be on at least a 10 percent shrinkage in volume (volume shrank on the retest by 25 percent). The market then had to close above the previous low (NYSE closed much higher than the July low). These conditions triggered a buy signal on the NYSE in October 2002. The volume method used was called "Low Volume Retest." (Refer to Chapter 4, Figure 4.1.)

Notice in March 2003 that the NYSE retested the July 2002 low on volume that was near 7.5 billion shares, which was 37.5 percent lighter than the volume at the July 2002 bottom. This resulted in a volume-method buy signal called "First Low Retest." (Refer to Chapter 4, Figure 4.10.) Since the volume on the March 2003 test of the July 2002 low was lighter than the October 2002 test of the July 2002 low, the March 2003 buy signal was stronger than the October 2002 buy signal. If you remember from Chapter 4, the lighter the volume on a retest of a previous swing, the stronger the buy signal.

As I said in Chapter 4, the higher the percentage decrease in volume on the retest of a previous high or low, the more reliable and stronger the signal will be for a reversal. That makes sense because if the energy is significantly less than at the previous high (or low), there will also be less force, which means a safer trade for a reversal.

Using Ord-Volume   Further volume analysis can be done with Ord-Volume. As you remember from Chapter 3, volume pushes price. The average daily volume in a leg of a stock or index denotes how much energy that leg has. By comparing the energy in the legs of an issue, a trader can identify which way the energy is pushing and can then direct his/her trading in the appropriate direction.

In Chapter 3, I also outlined a method for trading stocks using Ord-Volume, which is based on average daily volume. The trading method for indexes using the Ord-Volume method is slightly different. The average daily volume shrinkage in the legs of the indexes does not shrink as much as it does in stocks.

Let's review what I wrote in Chapter 3 regarding a buy signal for a stock triggered using the Ord-Volume method: A stock hits a minor new low and Ord-Volume shrinks by near 50 percent or greater against the previous down leg or previous up leg, and then closes above the previous low. Both conditions warrant the stock is in a strong position. This triggers the buy signal. Confirmation of a bottom is produced when Ord-Volume increases by 50 percent or more on the up leg after the bottom compared to the down leg going into the bottom.

A sell signal is triggered using the Ord-Volume method as follows: A stock hits a minor new high and the Ord-Volume on the current up leg shrinks by approximately 50 percent or greater compared with the Ord-Volume of the previous up leg or down leg; the stock then closes below the previous high. Both conditions determine the stock is in a weak position. This triggers the sell signal. Confirmation of a top is produced when Ord-Volume increases by 50 percent or more on the down leg after the top compared to the up leg going into the top.

Ord-Volume and Indexes   For indexes, for what every reason, their leg energy does not shrink that much between up and down legs. Instead, there is a more subtle energy shift in up and down legs. Traders can still identify turns in the indexes, but the shift in energy occurs to a much smaller degree. Therefore, a trader usually will not find a 50 percent decrease in Ord-Volume going into a low compared to the previous up leg or down leg. If, however, a trader did find an index with 50 percent shrinkage in a leg going into a low compared to the previous up leg or down leg, that would be a signal a trader should pay attention to as it is unusually strong and could lead to an important reversal.

Usually, a trader will not find leg energy shrinkage to this extreme in an index. What is more normal for the indexes is illustrated by the next example. I might add that the Ord-Volume buy and sell signal method for the indexes work much better for picking bottoms than it does for picking tops. Having said that, let's move on and look at the 2002 low for the NYSE and see how the Ord-Volume method performed.

Figure 9.6 displays the NYSE in Ord-Volume format starting from May 10, 2002, and running through November 22, 2002, which encompasses the first two lows in an important three-low formation. (We will look at the whole bottoming process in the Ord-Volume format for the NYSE in Figure 9.7.)

In Figure 9.6, I labeled each significant swing on the NYSE chart with a letter, starting at A and going to G. The first sign that the downtrend may have been ending on the NYSE came on the leg energy from swing B to swing C, which amounted to 2.1 billion shares. The down leg energy going into the B swing low came in at 1.55 billion shares. The up leg energy from B to C increased by 26 percent compared to the previous down leg energy from A to B, which suggested that the energy of the NYSE was starting to turn up in this time frame.

What followed was a mild consolidation from swing C to swing D, and then another rally leg started at swing D and rallied to swing E. The Ord-Volume for the leg rally from D to E came in at 1.37 billion shares,

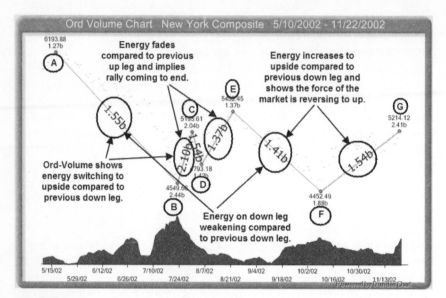

FIGURE 9.6 NYSE in Ord-Volume Format, Focusing on Two Lows in May and November 2002

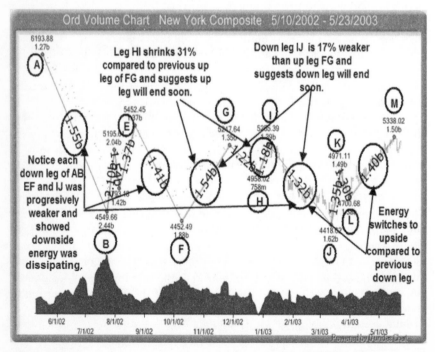

FIGURE 9.7 NYSE in Ord-Volume Format, Focusing on the Bottoming Period in 2002–2003

which was less than 35 percent of the Ord-Volume that was generated in the previous up leg from B to C. This volume decrease showed that the energy was fading and the market may fall back.

The market did fall back and the down leg that started at swing E and declined to swing F came in at 1.41 billion shares. This showed that volume for leg E to F was 9 percent weaker than the previous down leg from A to B, which had 1.55 billion shares. To keep a downtrend going, the energy in the current down leg should be at least equal to or higher than the previous down leg. This example of the current down leg energy decreasing by 9 percent compared to the previous down leg showed that the down force was weakening, which was a bullish condition for the market.

Another swing was put in at F, and the market rallied to swing G, creating a leg with volume of 1.54 billion shares, which was 9 percent stronger than the volume for the down leg from E to F of 1.41 billion shares. You can see that there was a shift of energy at swing F from down to up.

Let's move on to Figure 9.7, which is the NYSE still in the Ord-Volume format. Figure 9.7 of the NYSE starts in May 10, 2002, and runs into May 23, 2003, encompassing the whole bottoming process. This chart breaks up the bottoming process for the NYSE into two parts to show a clearer view of what went on and what story was told through the Ord-Volume method.

In Figure 9.7, the Ord-Volume for the up leg from H to I shrank by 31 percent compared to the previous up leg from F to G, which shows that the upside energy was waning and the market could reverse—which it did. However, the Ord-Volume for the down leg from I to J declined by 17 percent compared to the previous up leg from F to G, showing that there was still more force to the upside, which was bullish.

Signs of a Dissipating Downside Force Comparing the Ord-Volume in down legs of AB, EF and IJ, you can see that as the NYSE moved sideways from late July 2002 to early April 2003, each successive down leg shows less energy than the previous down leg. This was a sign that the downside force was dissipating, which was a bullish condition for the market.

As of late March 2003, the NYSE did not have the energy to push lower. At this point, either one of two things could occur: Either a sideways trading range would continue or a rally phase would start. I have noticed that, in the past, rallies for the indexes sometimes start with somewhat low Ord-Volume legs, but which are still higher than the previous Ord-Volume down leg that preceded the current up leg. I view this condition as the market being totally sold out and there is no selling pressure left; therefore, any buy at all sends the market higher.

The up leg from L and M showed an increase of Ord-Volume of 6 percent compared to the previous down leg of IJ, and this up leg started the bull market that last several more years. To summarize, bottoms form in the indexes when selling pressure dissipates to the extent that there is no energy left to push the market lower. The energy of each successive down leg is less than the energy of the previous down leg. Whether this takes two down legs or five, the last down leg should show the least amount of energy compare to the previous down legs.

Once the selling is totally exhausted then the uptrend can begin. The Ord-Volume method helps to identify the energy switch from down to up.

Momentum—Determining Direction and Velocity of Price Movement

Thus far, we have used sentiment analysis to determine longer-term and intermediate-term trends, as well as breadth and volume analyses. Momentum analysis completes the picture, giving traders the knowledge and confidence they need to invest successfully. Once traders find the correct direction of the market and trade in that direction, most everything will fall into place and the trader will have a greater chance of being successful.

A momentum indicator expresses the direction and velocity of price movement. Its purpose is to smooth out the bumps and wiggles of price action so a trader can more easily see and identify price direction. When a momentum indicator is rising, that issue is in an uptrend, and when the momentum indicator is declining, that issue is in a downtrend. I use weekly momentum indicators on the indexes because I believe they are useful for picking out trends that can last from three to six months and sometimes longer. Daily momentum indicators fluctuate too rapidly, which can possibly take a trader out of a long position too quickly on a minor consolidation.

The two weekly momentum indicators I like to use were reviewed in Chapter 6; they are the Price Momentum Oscillator (PMO) developed by Carl Swenlin and the moving average convergence/divergence (MACD) developed by Gerald Appel. Using momentum indicators it becomes relatively easy to see bullish and bearish crossover signals as they are triggered.

Both the PMO and MACD have two lines. When the lower line crosses above the upper line, a buy signal is triggered, and when the upper line crosses below the lower line a sell signal is triggered. There is no rocket science here; nevertheless, these indicators do serve an important function with regard to momentum and also help to confirm other indicators, which in the example of this chapter means volume and breadth analyses.

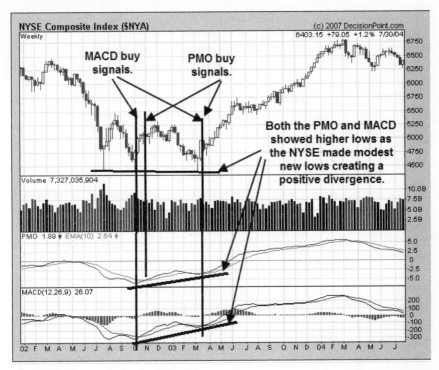

FIGURE 9.8   Momentum Indicators PMO and MACD on a Weekly Time Frame in the NYSE
Source: Chart courtesy of DecisionPoint.com.

Figure 9.8 shows the major bottom put in during 2002–2003 on the NYSE, using PMO and MACD momentum indicators on a weekly time frame. The bottom window in Figure 9.8 is the MACD indicator and the second window up from the bottom is the PMO indicator.

A bullish crossover and buy signal on the MACD indicator appeared in early October 2002, and in early November 2002 a bullish crossover and buy signal was triggered on the PMO. The market rallied several weeks and came back down in March 2003, testing the lows of July and October 2002.

Another important aspect of momentum indicators is divergence. Notice in Figure 9.8 that both PMO and MACD were much higher than their previous lows while the NYSE was testing its previous low. This condition shows that momentum was rising when the NYSE was matching its previous lows. This created a bullish divergence and would have bolstered a trader's confidence for a bullish bottom outcome.

Then, in mid-March 2003 both the PMO and MACD had bullish crossovers again, triggering buy signals. Most momentum indicators do have a small degree of lag time after tops and bottoms for signals to be triggered. Still, they are great tools to help confirm other indicators to keep traders in a trend.

In Figure 9.9, notice that both the weekly PMO and MACD gave bullish signals in March 2003. The market then trended higher into March 2004 before bearish crossovers occurred. Since both weekly PMO and MACD indicators were rising during that time span, traders would have remained long for a very profitable position.

Thus far, we have examined the signals at the 2002–2003 bottom in the NYSE using the three confirmation tools of breadth, volume, and momentum analyses. The more tools traders use to confirm or deny a turn in the market the higher the percentage of success of being correct.

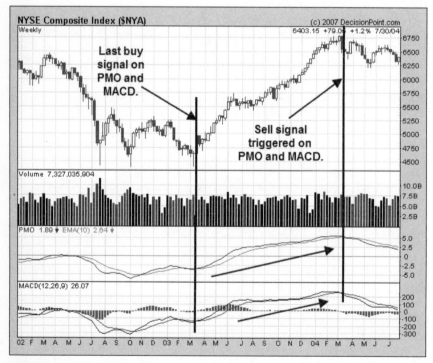

FIGURE 9.9   PMO and MACD Generate Bullish Signals in March 2003 that Last until March 2004
Source: Chart courtesy of DecisionPoint.com.

STEP 3: PICKING THE STRONGEST SECTORS

Having identified the bottom in 2002–2003 on the NYSE (thus putting the wind at our backs), the next step is to select two or three of the strongest sectors. By concentrating on a couple of the strongest sectors, traders are able to capitalize on percentage returns for their investment dollars. That is the only reason to be in the market: to make the highest return with the lowest risk possible.

Reviewing Sectors Analysis

To review from Chapter 2, a sector is a group of stocks in the same industry, such as banks, semiconductors, energy, and so forth. Before trying to pick the strongest stocks in the market, an easier step is to identify a couple of the strongest sectors in the market and then pick the best-performing stocks within those sectors. As I wrote in Chapter 2, this two-step process will get you closer to your goal of picking the strongest stock, more quickly and easily. There are thousands upon thousands of stocks, and picking the one that is likely to appreciate the most is a monumental task. However, there are only 36 or so sectors, depending on how the sectors are broken down. Therefore, picking a couple of strong sectors out of 36 is a much more manageable task.

Sector strength can be identified by studying what happens to that sector in a declining NYSE market. Strong sectors will drop less on a percentage basis compared with weak sectors; therefore, the sectors that hold up the best during a decline should perform the best when the next rally phase begins.

Let's take a look at the major bottom on the NYSE in 2002–2003, examining the nine sectors (as used by John Murphy, chief technical analyst of Stockcharts.com) of banks, gold and silver, semiconductors, oil services, pharmaceuticals, S&P 500 retail, Internet, biotech, and brokers. These sectors provide a good cross-section of the economy. These nine sectors are displayed together graphically so that a trader can see the performance of each compared to the others in the same time frame.

The strongest sectors that held up the best going into the major low of 2002–2003 are near the top of the chart and the weakest sector going into that low appear near the bottom. Figure 9.10 is the comparison chart of the nine sectors going into the major low of 2002 and 2003. You will notice that gold and silver ($XAU) and brokers ($XBD) held up the best; Internet ($DOT) and semiconductors ($SOX) were the worst. Therefore, at the major low in 2002–2003, a trader should have picked stocks that

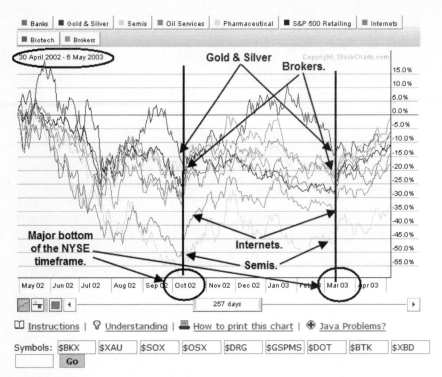

FIGURE 9.10   Sector Comparison at 2002–2003 low in the NYSE
Source: Chart courtesy of StockCharts.com.

were in the gold and silver and brokers sectors and avoided stocks in the internet and semiconductors sectors.

Looking ahead, let's test the outcome of our sector analysis. Figure 9.11 shows how these sectors performed going into the next high in March 2004.

The first strong sector we identified as of the 2002–2003 low was the gold and silver index, which was off 10 percent as of the March 2003 low. Gold and silver ended up 30 percent at the March 2004 high, for a net gain of 40 percentage points. The brokers sector was also strong at the low, and was off 10 percent as of March 2003. It ended up 50 percent at the March 2004 high, for a net gain of 60 percentage points.

By comparison, the Internet sector was a weak sector and was off 30 percent at the March 2003 low. It ended up 20 percent at the March 2004 high for a next gain of 50 percentage points, which was pretty good comeback for a weak sector. The semiconductor sector was off 40 percent at the March 2003 low and ended down 10 percent at the March 2004 high, for a next gain of 30 percentage points, and was the worst performer of

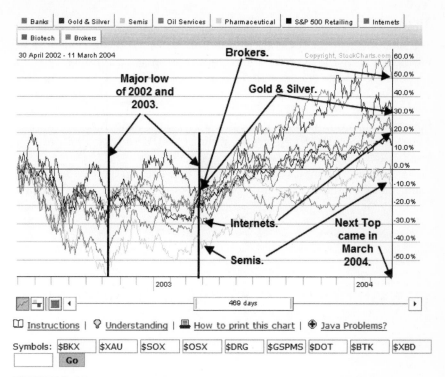

■ Banks ■ Gold & Silver ■ Semis ■ Oil Services ■ Pharmaceutical ■ S&P 500 Retailing ■ Internets
■ Biotech ■ Brokers

30 April 2002 - 11 March 2004

Brokers.

Copyright, StockCharts.com

60.0%
50.0%

Major low of 2002 and 2003.

Gold & Silver.

40.0%
30.0%
20.0%
10.0%
0.0%
-10.0%
-20.0%

Internets.

Next Top came in March 2004.

-30.0%
-40.0%
-50.0%

Semis.

2003
2004

469 days

📖 Instructions | 💡 Understanding | 🖥 How to print this chart | ⊕ Java Problems?

Symbols: $BKX | $XAU | $SOX | $OSX | $DRG | $GSPMS | $DOT | $BTK | $XBD

Go

FIGURE 9.11 Sector Performance Going into Next High in March 2004
Source: Chart courtesy of StockCharts.com.

this nine-sector grouping. In this particular example—given the magnitude of the market low—if a trader bought at the right time, it would appear he or she would have been profitable no matter what was bought. The point, however, is that by identifying the sectors that hold up the best at a market low, traders will increase the probability of a positive outcome when the market turns and begins to rally.

STEP 4: SELECTING THE STRONGEST STOCKS

Now that we have identified the strongest sectors, the final step is stock analysis and stock selection. Based on sector analysis, we have determined that gold and silver and brokers were the two strongest sectors going into the 2002–2003 low. Therefore, we will concentrate on purchasing stocks in those two sectors.

Analyzing Stocks within a Strong Sector

The same strength analysis that was performed for the sectors will be done for the stocks in those sectors. In the gold and silver sector, I have picked 10 stocks to conduct the comparison analysis (which is the same as what we performed for the sectors). The stocks are Freeport McMoran (FCX), Aqnico Eagle Mines (AEM), Meridian Gold (MDG), Goldcorp. (GG), Barrick Gold Corporation (ABX), Silver Standard Resources (SSRI), Pan American Silver (PAAS), Newmont Mining (NEM), Kinross Gold Corporation (KGC), and Harmony Gold Mining (HMY).

As Figure 9.12 shows, the two stocks that held up the best especially going into the March 2003 low were Freeport McMoran and Goldcorp. Freeport McMoran started up 20 percent from the March 2003 low and

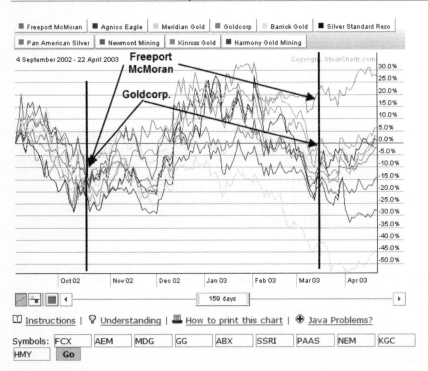

FIGURE 9.12   Comparison of Performance of Stocks in the Gold Sector
Source: Chart courtesy of StockCharts.com.

continued to rally to March 2004 where it was up 200 percent—making a 190 percentage point gain in that time frame.

Goldcorp started at near even as of the March 2003 low and rallied about 30 percent at the March 2004 high for a net gain of 30 percentage points. However, as Figure 9.13 shows, there were other gold stocks that did better than Goldcorp, but you still would have been a winner. This method still proved effective as this comparison did identify one of the rocket stocks, which was Freeport McMoran up 190 percent.

Moving to the next strong sector, brokerage, we concentrate on 10 stocks. They are: AG Edwards (AGE), Lehman (LEH), Morgan Stanley (MS), Raymond James (RJF), Legg Mason (LM), TD Ameritrade (AMTD), E*Trade (ETFC), Morgan Stanley (MS), Bear Stearns (BSC), and Merrill Lynch (MER). Figure 9.14 displays these 10 stocks together, providing a visual representation of the best performers.

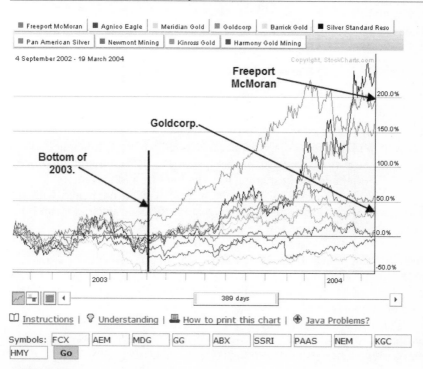

FIGURE 9.13   Performance of Gold Stocks Going into March 2004 High
Source: Chart courtesy of StockCharts.com.

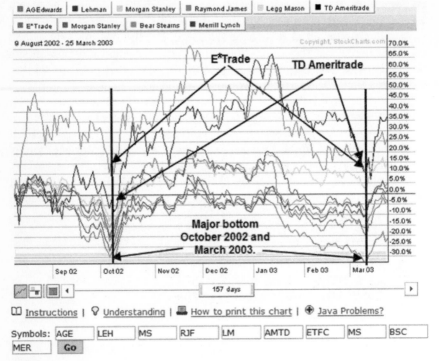

FIGURE 9.14 Comparison of 10 Brokerage Stocks at the 2002–2003 Market Bottom
Source: Chart courtesy of StockCharts.com.

Notice that in this comparison analysis (Figure 9.14) it is much easier to identify the two strongest brokerage stocks, E*Trade and TD Ameritrade. They held up the best going into the lows by a long shot.

Turning to Figure 9.15, let's take a look at what happened with the two stocks we identified as the strongest performers within a strong sector, as of a major market low.

As Figure 9.15 shows, E*Trade started up 10 percent from the March 2003 low and rallied to the March 2004 high up 310 percent, for a net gain of 300 percentage points. TD Ameritrade also started up 10 percent from the March 2003 low and rallied to March 2004 up 350 percent, for a net gain of 340 percentage points.

For further confirmation of buy and sell signals for individual stocks, we conducted an Ord-Volume study on TD Ameritrade (AMTD) as the market was making a low back in 2002 (see Figure 9.16).

PerfChart
(AGE,LEH,MS,RJF,LM,AMTD,ETFC,MS,BSC,MER)
Interactive Performance Comparison Chart

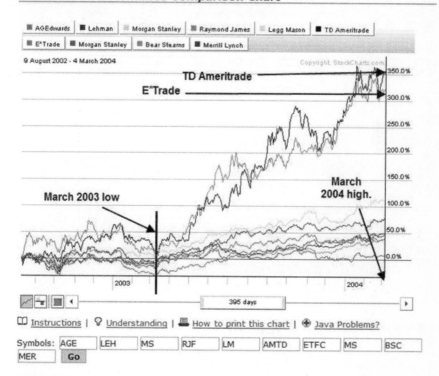

FIGURE 9.15 Performance of Brokerage Stocks Going into the March 2004 High
Source: Chart courtesy of StockCharts.com.

AMTD generated a buy signal using the Ord-Volume method in October 2001 with a close above $3.75. A trading range developed after the buy signal, followed by another test of the low in July 2002 before AMTD started its massive rally.

Now, looking at the mid-2002 time frame, notice how Ord-Volume on the down leg to $2.95 was 760,000 shares. But after that low was put in, energy reversed to the upside—and Ord-Volume saw a huge expansion to 1.75 million shares as the rally began, which would take this stock up to $8.93 by mid-2003.

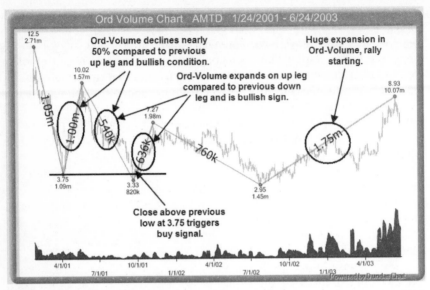

FIGURE 9.16   Ord-Volume Format Study of TD Ameritrade at the 2002 Market Low

PUTTING IT ALL TOGETHER

To be successful, traders need a variety of tools to identify and confirm signals in the market. It's not enough to act on what looks like a buy signal or to hear about a "hot stock" that sounds promising. It takes patience, discipline, and, most of all, dedication.

Like most traders, I had to learn this the hard way. As I shared in the opening chapter about my own journey to becoming a trader, I had to make all the mistakes that comprise the early phases of a learning curve. I started off thinking that I could do this easily, only to be proven wrong. There is nothing easy about the market.

It is possible, however, to study the movements of the market using fairly logical methods. The foundation of my methodology is the top-down approach. I start with the biggest, broadest picture possible, which is the overall market. Once I determine which way the wind is blowing, shall we say, in the market, I know whether I want to be trading from the long side or not—or if I want to initiate short trades, if that is my style.

When I am convinced that my plan is in sync with the broader market, I know that I have the "wind at my back," and my chances for a successful trade just went up dramatically. From there, my trading technique moves through the steps I outlined in this chapter, from the overall trend, to sector analysis, and then stock picking.

In every chapter, I have emphasized the importance of volume. It bears repeating: Rather than focus on price alone, traders need to look at volume as it displays—and sometimes loudly and clearly—what is really going on in the market. To give an example, a stock may rally several points, but if the volume is thin compared with previous moves, then how reliable is that upward move? It's like getting a little burst of speed out of a car as it's running out of gas. You're not going to get very far before it stalls and then stops.

Volume reveals the energy within the up and down legs of a stock or index. When there is increasing volume (energy) in successive up or down moves, you can see quite clearly which way the trend is going. When volume dissipates as the market moves lower, and then the volume picks up on the up legs, you know that that the tide is turning. The energy has shifted to the upside.

My purpose in this book is not to tell you everything there is to know about technical analysis, but rather to share with you some of my tried-and-true methods, techniques, and indicators that have helped me over the years. This is how I trade the market, with a methodical approach that confirms what I see and provides me confidence at every step.

Now I turn it over to you. By tackling the market sequentially—going from the top down—you, too, can increase your probability of making a successful trade by identifying the trend, picking the strongest sectors, and focusing on the best stocks within those sectors. As a result, you will know not only what to trade that has the best probability of success, but also why you made that trade.

The market never ceases to fascinate me, and I feel very fortunate that I have been able to make my living as a trader. I cannot sit back on my past performance, however, and neither can you.

To trade, you must be a lifelong student of the market. Just as I had to study the market in the beginning to find out where I went wrong, I have become a committed student to listen to what the market is telling me at any given moment. It's all there—in the patterns, the volume, and the analysis. It takes time, and it takes patience. The rewards, however, are yours for the reaping.

Index